Melissa Leapman's
knitting beyond
scarves

Melissa Leapman's
knitting beyond
scarves

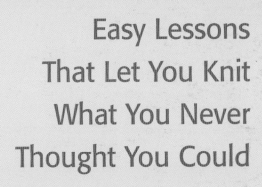

Easy Lessons
That Let You Knit
What You Never
Thought You Could

Watson-Guptill Publications
New York

Senior Acquisitions Editor: Joy Aquilino
Project Editor: Andrea Curley
Art Director: Elizabeth Elsas Mandel
Book Designer: Areta Buk/Thumb Print
Production Manager: Ellen Greene
Technical Editor: Charlotte Quiggle
Photographer: Donald Scott
Technical illustrations: Carmen Galiano
Schematic illustrations: Melissa Leapman

First published in 2006 by Watson-Guptill Publications,
a division of VNU Business Media, Inc.,
770 Broadway, New York, N.Y. 10003
www.watsonguptill.com

Library of Congress Cataloging-in-Publication Data

Leapman, Melissa.
[Knitting beyond scarves]
Melissa Leapman's knitting beyond scarves : easy lessons that let you knit
what you never thought you could. — 1st ed.
p. cm.
title: Knitting beyond scarves
Includes bibliographical references and index.
ISBN 0-8230-2614-0 (978-0-8230-2614-2)
1. Knitting—Patterns. I. Title. II. Title: Knitting beyond scarves.
TT820.L380 2006
746.43'2042—dc22

2006012955

Manufactured in Singapore

First printing, 2006

1 2 3 4 5 6 7 8 9 /14 13 12 11 10 09 08 07 06

TO JOY

ACKNOWLEDGMENTS
Special thanks go to the following knitters who helped to make the sample projects photographed in this book: Lynn Gates, Cindy Grosch, Barbara Hillery, Cheryl Keeley, Ilene Levine, JoAnn Moss, Joan Murphy, Pam Porter, Norma Jean Sternschein, and Rusty Slabinski.

I am grateful to George Timmons for allowing our photography crew to set up shop in his home.

As usual, editors Joy Aquilino and Andrea Curley professionally—and lovingly—helped to transform my working idea for this book into what you see here. Thank you!

I am especially grateful to have had another lucky opportunity to work with Charlotte Quiggle as my technical editor. Her knowledge and experience have greatly improved this book. (In addition, her early working habits made the office water cooler a much friendlier place in the wee hours!)

Thank you, too, Scarlet and Phil Taylor for such extraordinary generosity during our photo shoot in beautiful Wilmington, North Carolina. Every author (and human being!) should have such wonderful friends!

contents

introduction

DO YOU LOVE TO KNIT—OR WISH YOU KNEW HOW?

Have you mastered the basic techniques of casting on, the knit stitch, and binding off? Now, be honest, how many of those simple skinny scarves have *you* knit out of today's novelty yarns? If you're like most avid, new knitters, you've probably created enough to wear a different one every day of the week (not to mention the dozens you've made as gifts. . . .)!

YOUR KNITTING GOALS (AND DREAMS!)

Eventually, though, you'll want to add to your knitting (and fashion!) repertoire. Are you ready to learn new skills, build your knitter's know-how, and progress to making other fun fashion items?

HOW YOU'LL ACHIEVE THEM

Drawing on my experience teaching workshops to thousands of crafters across the country every year, in this book I offer a series of step-by-step instructions for basic knitting skills that will help you learn, build on, and expand your knitting knowledge. Each section of technical information presents and explores a different knitting technique. Clear illustrations show every knitting maneuver, and user-friendly "Knit Notes" sections offer help for common knitting problems.

Each lesson is followed by one or two projects that are specifically designed to hone your new skills. I've included advice and tips in every pattern that will help you navigate any unusual or complex parts of the project, so it will almost

be like having your own personal knitting coach sitting right there beside you on your sofa!

WHERE YOU'LL BE

Imagine knitting a beautiful variegated hat or suede-like fringed shoulder bag as a near beginner! And you only need to learn a few simple skills to create a sexy, off-the-shoulder pullover or soft, tie-front cardigan.

How is this possible? Well, rather than show you tons of basic stitches and techniques all at once, I've presented the techniques a little at a time, with plenty of coordinating projects to help you practice and showcase your new skills. That way, you'll be able to exploit and expand on your knowledge of knitting sooner—plus you'll get the instant gratification of creating fashionable designs. Work through this book sequentially and you'll be making the most of the skills you already possess or have just learned, *and* knitting a much more interesting and challenging variety of projects than you ever thought possible. Plus, special designer details such as fully-fashioned shaping—making your increases and decreases in from the edge of the fabric where instructed—will allow you to knit more stylish and body-conscious garments.

ENJOY THE PROCESS

Join me on this fun knitting adventure. As you progress from one easy lesson to the next, you'll be building a collection of skills—and a great new wardrobe!

HAPPY KNITTING!

entry-level knitting

Here you'll learn the knitting basics—everything from the various tools and supplies you'll need to the most common stitch in this needle art, the knit stitch, as well as how to navigate a knitting pattern. Let's get started!

Knitting Supplies

Before you start to knit, you should gather together all the materials and tools you'll need. This way you won't have to go searching for things while you're stitching!

YARN

Now is such a fun and exciting time to be a knitter. Thousands of beautiful yarns are available on the market these days, from soft and cozy wools to crisp and colorful cottons, to versatile machine-washable acrylics. Luckily for us, manufacturers follow fashion trends pretty closely, allowing us to duplicate—and often improve upon!—ready-to-wear offerings in the latest colors and textures, with our own hands.

Before starting any project, be sure to read the yarn label. It contains the following important information:

- **Fiber Content** This information describes the material the yarn is made out of, such as cotton, wool, alpaca, or acrylic.
- **Yardage** This helps you decide how much yarn to buy to complete a particular project.
- **Yarn Weight** This term refers to the diameter of the strand of yarn. Bulky yarns knit up more quickly than finer ones and require less yardage for the same size project.
- **Suggested Knitting Gauge** This information tells you what size knitting needles the yarn manufacturer recommends for the specific yarn, as well as the number of stitches that will result per inch (or often over 4").
- **Laundering Instructions** This suggests how to care properly for your finished item.
- Also, look for the **Dye Lot Number** on the label. Since each color of any particular yarn is dyed in batches, color variations occur between dye lots. When purchasing yarn for a project, be sure it's all from the same dye lot. Otherwise, parts of your completed item may have subtle (but usually quite noticeable) color differences.

To avoid the disappointment and hassle of running out of yarn in the middle of a project, always buy extra. Just ask any knitter: you can never have too much yarn!

Knit Notes

Yarn is often sold in hanks (loosely tied bundles) rather than skeins or balls. Before you can use the yarn, you must wind it into balls. To make this process easier, position two chairs back to back and drape the hank over the two backs to keep it from tangling. Other options are to enlist a volunteer willing to hold the hank over his or her outstretched arms or to use an umbrella yarn swift (available at yarn stores). *Slowly* unwind the yarn, carefully undoing any tangles you encounter, and form a soft, loosely wound ball. If you come to a knot, cut it out and begin a new ball. Be sure not to wind the yarn too tightly or else you'll stretch the fibers.

Yarn Choice and Substitution

With all the yummy yarns available on the market these days, you might want to change the yarn you use for a particular pattern—but be careful!

Each project in this collection was designed with a specific yarn in mind. Due to unique characteristics such as fiber content, twist, texture, and thickness, every yarn appears and behaves differently when knitted. For the best results, I recommend that you use the suggested yarn.

However, if you would like to make a yarn substitution, you can. But be sure to choose one whose size and weight match the one designated in the pattern. As I mentioned in the last section, yarn sizes and weights are usually printed on the label. But for an accurate test, knit a test swatch

Knit Notes

When making yarn substitutions, it's a good idea to keep the original yarn's fiber content in mind. The "Big Easy Jacket" on page 90, for example, is worked in a super bulky weight yarn that's a wool and acrylic blend. If you were to mistakenly choose a 100% cotton yarn of that same thickness instead, the sheer weight of the knitted fabric would cause your jacket to grow uncontrollably in length!

YARN SIZE AND WEIGHT	DESCRIPTION	STITCHES PER 4"
Super Fine	Fingering weight (some of the thinnest kinds of hand-knitting yarns available)	27 or more
Fine	Sport weight	23–26 sts
Light	DK weight	21–24 sts
Medium	Worsted weight	16–20 sts
Bulky	Bulky weight	12–15 sts
Super Bulky	Super Bulky weight (some of the thickest kinds of hand-knitting yarns available)	11 or fewer sts

with the yarn you prefer, using the needle size suggested on the ball band. Make the swatch at least 4" square.

Now count the total number of stitches over 4" width-wise on your swatch and use the table above to determine its weight. If, for example, your knitted piece has 20 stitches over 4", your yarn is "worsted"—or "medium"—weight.

NEEDLES

So, you've gone shopping, petted every single yarn in the store, and brought home your absolute favorite. Now you'll need some tools.

Needles are the basic tools of knitting, and they're available in three shapes.

- **Single-point knitting needles** are the most common type. The knob on one end prevents stitches from falling off, and the point on the other end allows you to work up stitches and then move them easily from one needle to the other. For comfort and speed, choose the shortest length that will accommodate the number of stitches you'll be knitting.
- **Circular knitting needles** consist of two knitting needle points connected by a cable. They are most often used for knitting in the round (knitting without seams), though many knitters, myself included, enjoy working with them even when knitting back and forth on flat pieces. The long cable between the two needle points helps to distribute the stitches—and the weight of the fabric—evenly while knitting, causing less stress and strain on the body.
- **Double-pointed knitting needles** are short, straight needles with points on both ends. Usually packaged in sets of four or five, they are used when knitting pieces in the round that have small circumferences, such as socks, sleeves, and mittens.

Knitting needle circumference determines the size of your knitted stitches. Needles with smaller circumferences (for example, size 4/3.50 mm) result in tighter stitches; larger needles (such as size 10/6.00 mm) yield bigger, looser ones. Metric sizes are often indicated, too, which allows for more precise, less subjective measurements.

OTHER KNITTING TOOLS

Other items will come in handy as you knit, including:

Scissors to snip yarn at the completion of a project or to even out fringe and tassels for a professional-looking finish
Tape measure to measure your knitted fabric accurately
Blunt yarn needles with large eyes to sew seams without piercing individual strands that comprise the yarn
Pointed-end yarn needle to attach woven fabric linings and zipper tapes
Safety pins to mark specific stitches or to hold a single live stitch until it is worked again
Straight pins to hold project pieces together temporarily while seaming
Stitch markers to indicate a particular stitch or place in the pattern (the beginning of the armhole, for example)
Closed-ring marker to separate groups of live stitches (stitches that are being worked) when placed between them on the knitting needle
Stitch holders to hold groups of live, working stitches temporarily until they are worked again
Row counter to help keep track of the number of rows knitted
Crochet hooks to pick up dropped stitches
Paper and pencil to make notes as you work a pattern
And last but not least, a **sturdy (not to mention roomy) knitting bag** to keep all your knitting yarns and tools organized and ready to go whenever you are!

Getting Started

Have you assembled everything you need? Are you ready? Then let's begin!

MAKING A SLIP KNOT

The first stitch of nearly every piece of knitted fabric is a slip knot. Its adjustable loop makes it a perfect fit for any size knitting needle. Here's how to make it.

1 Begin approximately 6" from the end of the yarn, wrap the yarn into a looped circle, and then place the working yarn (the yarn coming from the ball) beneath the loop (see illustration 1).

2 Use your knitting needle to scoop up the strand of yarn coming from the ball and pull it through the center of the loop (see illustration 2).

3 Tighten the slip knot by pulling on both ends of yarn at the same time. Be sure not to make the slip knot too tight. It should hug your knitting needle but still slide easily (see illustration 3).

Now wasn't that easy?

HOLDING THE YARN AND NEEDLES

There are as many ways of holding the yarn and needles as there are folks who knit! Following are instructions for the two most common methods.

Like any new motor skill, controlling the yarn and the needles as you knit can feel awkward at first, so be patient. Try both methods and choose the one that feels more comfortable to you. You might even discover that you find your own personal way! There's no right or wrong way to knit; the important thing is that you hold your yarn and needles so that you can control the tension (the size of the stitches you create).

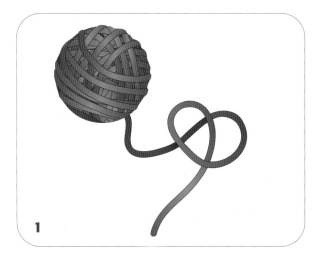

1

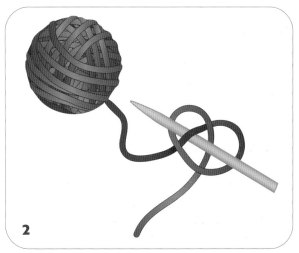

2

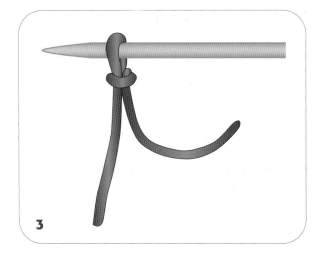

3

The English Method

In this method of knitting, the yarn is wrapped, or "thrown," over the needles with your right hand.

1 Place one knitting needle in your left hand and then position the working yarn around the fingers of your right hand as shown (see illustration 1 below).

2 Hold the other knitting needle in your right hand, positioning it as you would a knife. Use your right index finger to control the tension of the working yarn (see illustration 2 below).

3 Some knitters prefer to hold the right-hand needle as if it were a pencil (see illustration 3 left). However, this method tends to cause additional strain on the hand, particularly when knitting with heavier yarns.

The Continental Method

Although knitting is not a race (well, not unless you're in one of my workshops across the country), many people find this method of holding the yarn and needles faster since there's less hand movement involved.

1 Wrap the working yarn around the fingers of your left hand as shown (see illustration 1 below).

2 Place one needle in your left hand, using your left index finger to control the tension of the yarn (see illustration 2 below).

3 Place the other knitting needle—the working needle—in your right hand.

Use the method most comfortable for you.

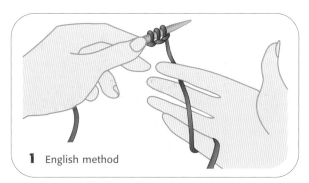

1 English method

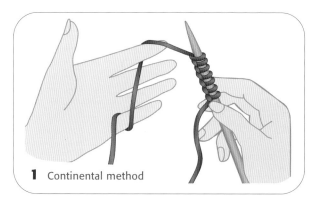

1 Continental method

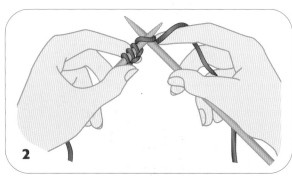

2

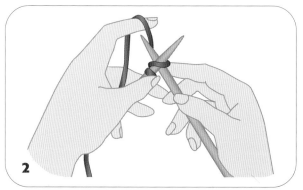

2

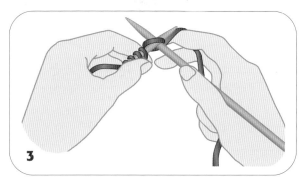

3

Knit Notes

If you're left-handed, don't bother to reverse these knitting maneuvers. Knitting is a two-handed activity, just like typing. If you learn the same yarn and needle positions as most other knitters, you won't have to worry later about making adjustments to patterns.

THE CABLE CAST ON

Okay, you now have one stitch ready to go on your knitting needle. The next step is to add more stitches.

There are many ways to cast on, or place stitches on, the needle to begin knitting. The cable cast on is one of my favorites: it's simple to do, easy to remember, and creates a lovely, cordlike edge.

1 Begin by making a slip knot (see page 13). Place the needle holding the slip knot in your left hand. Insert the point of your right-hand knitting needle *knitwise* (from front to back) into the slip knot and then bring the working yarn between the two needles from back to front (see illustration 1).

2 Use the right-hand needle to scoop up the loop of yarn you've created (see illustration 2).

3 Place this new stitch onto the left-hand needle, twisting the stitch by inserting the left-hand needle *from the front*. One new stitch has been cast on!

Knit Notes

Twisting each stitch as you transfer it from the right- to the left-hand needle while casting on tightens the loop slightly and creates a sturdy (not to mention beautiful!) cord-like finish on the cast-on edge.

4 To cast on another stitch, insert the point of your right-hand needle *between* the first and second stitches on the left-hand needle rather than directly into the first stitch, wrap the working yarn between the two needles from back to front, and complete the new stitch as before (see illustration 3).

Try to use an even tension, keeping the yarn flowing smoothly and easily through your fingers, so that all your cast-on stitches will be approximately the same size. Be sure not to cast on too tightly by pulling too hard on the yarn, or else your first row of knitting will be unnecessarily frustrating and your piece of fabric will be narrower than you want it to be. (Don't ask me how I know . . . .)

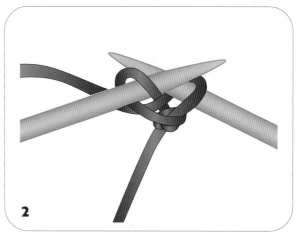

MAKING THE KNIT STITCH

The most basic stitch in knitting is the knit stitch. From the front, this stitch appears smooth and looks like a "V"; from the back, it's bumpy. (And as you progress through the following lessons, you'll be amazed at what you can do with just this one basic stitch!)

1 To make a knit stitch, place the needle with the cast-on stitches in your left hand. Hold the empty needle in your right hand.

Keeping the working yarn to the back, position the tip of the right-hand needle *beneath* the left-hand needle. Insert the tip of the right-hand needle into the first stitch on the left-hand needle *from front to back* (see illustration 1).

2 Wrap the working yarn from right to left, under and over the point of the right-hand needle (see illustration 2).

3 Use the right-hand needle to scoop the yarn and pull it through the first stitch on the left-hand needle (see illustration 3).

4 Drop the first stitch off the left-hand needle and leave the new knit stitch on the right-hand needle (see illustration 4).

To complete the row of knit stitches, repeat these steps until the left-hand needle is empty.

Congratulations—you're knitting!

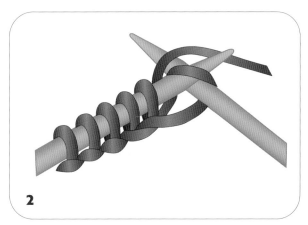

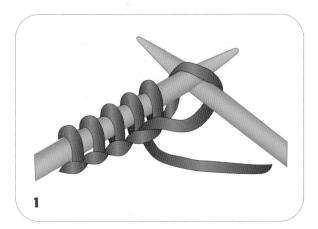

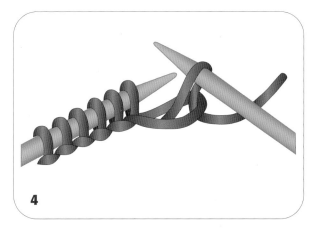

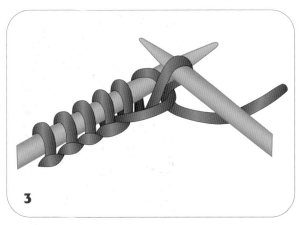

Basic Finishing Techniques

So, you're on the last row of your piece of knitting. Now what?

BINDING OFF

Binding off is the technique that links together live stitches so that they don't unravel when they're removed from the knitting needles. It is used to end a piece of fabric but can also be used to create shaping within knitted projects (for an armhole or to begin a neckline, for instance) or to make buttonholes or other special finishes.

Once you've finished knitting a piece of fabric (or have gotten to an area that will be shaped by getting rid of several stitches all at once), the pattern will tell you to bind off. To bind off, begin by knitting two stitches *loosely*. Use the tip of your left-hand needle to pull the first knitted stitch over the second one, removing this bound-off stitch from the right-hand needle (see illustration 1).

To bind off another stitch, knit one more stitch, then use the tip of the left-hand needle to pull the second stitch on the right-hand needle over the first one. Repeat these steps for each additional stitch being bound off.

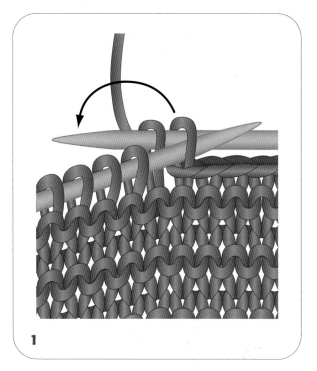

1

Knit Notes

Notice that in order to bind off one stitch, two stitches must be knitted. To keep track of stitches when binding off, count the stitches that are being bound off *as you pull them over and off the right-hand needle* rather than as you're knitting them!

FASTENING OFF

Fastening off (or as it's sometimes called, finishing off) is the last step done after binding off. It secures the fabric so it won't unravel.

To end a piece of knitting when there's one stitch left, simply cut the yarn, leaving a 6" tail. Then pull the tail tightly through the remaining loop (see illustration 2).

2

WEAVING IN YARN TAILS TO HIDE THEM

When beginning and ending a piece of knitting (and also whenever you attach a new ball of yarn), I've told you to be sure to leave a 6" tail of yarn. After the knitting is completed, what do you do with the tails? You can't just cut them off, because they will poke out onto the right side of the fabric, or worse yet, come undone, allowing your precious knitting to unravel!. Instead, you'll weave in these ends on the wrong side of the fabric, securing them so they won't pop out. Here's how to do it.

1 Use a pointed-end yarn needle and make short running stitches on the wrong side of the fabric in a diagonal line for about 1" or so, piercing the yarn strands that comprise the stitches. Make sure that these stitches don't show on the right side of the fabric (see illustration 1).

2 Then work back to where you began, going alongside your previous running stitches (see illustration 2).

3 Finally, to secure the tail, work another stitch or two, this time actually piercing the stitches you just created (see illustration 3).

4 Cut the yarn close to the fabric.

BLOCKING

Blocking is a finishing process that helps "set" your project pieces to the desired size prior to seaming. It serves to even out the stitches, making the overall fabric look, well, beautiful and professionally knit.

There are several ways to block, but here are two common methods.

■ **Wet-blocking** Launder the knitted pieces, being sure to follow the manufacturer's instructions on the yarn label. Lay the pieces flat on a padded surface away from direct sunlight, patting them gently to your desired measurements (usually given in a schematic illustration in the pattern). Pin down the damp fabric (using rustless pins!) and wait for the pieces to dry.

■ **Steam-blocking** Place a damp cloth over each piece and carefully run a steam iron just above it. *Don't touch the fabric with the hot iron or else you might damage it by flattening or even melting it!*

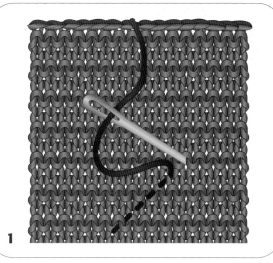

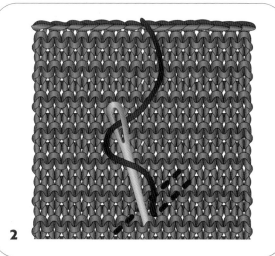

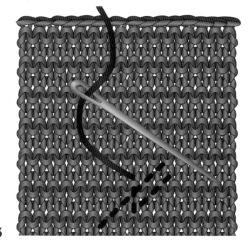

WHIPSTITCH SEAM

After you've blocked your knitted fabric, you'll often need to assemble pieces together to complete a project. The order in which seams should be sewn is indicated in the "Finishing" section of each pattern. If your project is a sweater, you can refer to the specific Sweater Assembly Illustration on page 126 to see how the pieces fit together.

The whipstitch seam is easy to learn and uses an overcast stitch to join two pieces of fabric. The stitching of this seam is always done in the same direction following a spiraling path, going down from front to back on one piece of fabric and then down from back to front on the second piece.

1 Lay both pieces of fabric flat with their right sides up.

2 Pin your pieces together on both side edges, as well as a few times in the middle of the fabric. You don't want your pieces to be mismatched!

3 Thread a blunt-tip yarn needle with your sewing yarn (usually the same yarn you've knitted your project with).

4 Insert the needle *from front to back* through one piece of fabric and then *from back to front* through the corresponding stitch of the second piece of fabric (see illustration below).

5 Continue in this way, trying to maintain an even tension with the sewing yarn as you stitch.

Knit Notes

If your fabric was knitted in a particularly hairy or fragile yarn, use a strong, smooth yarn in a coordinating color to sew your seams. It'll make the finishing faster and easier (and keep you, the knitter, much happier)!

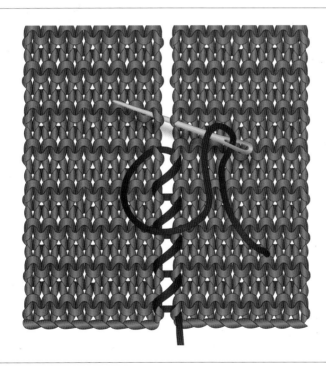

Oops! Fixing Common Mistakes, Part One

A necessary part of acquiring any new skill is learning how to recover from errors. If you glance down and notice a problem with your fabric, don't rip it all out! Before you do anything, just take a deep breath—it's likely that you can fix the mistake without having to start over from the beginning. This section will show you how.

CORRECTING A DROPPED KNIT STITCH

Occasionally a knit stitch may drop off your knitting needle without you noticing it immediately. When this happens, you can place it back onto your needle without too much trouble.

1 If one stitch has unraveled down a single row, position the knitting so that the dropped stitch is toward the back of the fabric and the loose yarn is toward the front (see illustration 1).

2 Insert the right-hand knitting needle *from back to front* through the dropped stitch and then under the loose yarn (see illustration 2).

3 Use the left-hand needle to lift the dropped stitch *over* the loose strand of yarn and off the right-hand needle (see illustration 3).

4 Slip the new stitch that's on the right-hand needle back onto the left-hand needle. When transferring the stitch, be sure to insert the left-hand needle into it from front to back and from left to right (see illustration 4).

If more than one stitch has been dropped, fix them one at a time.

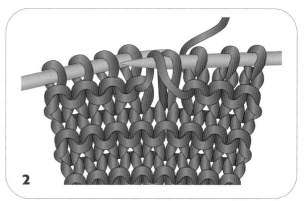

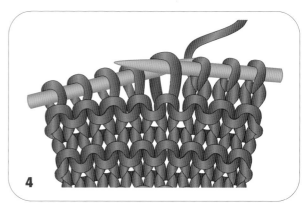

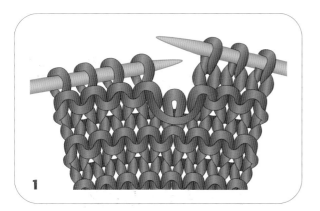

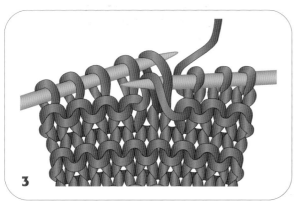

UNRAVELING STITCHES TO RIP OUT A PARTIAL ROW

Occasionally, you will need to rip out a row of your knitting one stitch at a time. Don't worry—it's really not that hard!

To unravel a stitch, place the working yarn to the back, then insert the left-hand needle into the first stitch on the right-hand needle one row below the live stitch that's sitting on the needle (see illustration 1).

Slide the tip of the right-hand needle back, let the loop drop from the needle, and pull on the working yarn to unravel the stitch.

UNRAVELING STITCHES TO RIP OUT AN ENTIRE ROW

If you must rip out a whole row (or more!) of stitches, just remove the knitting needle and tug on the working yarn. If you're removing multiple rows, stop with the row above the offending row, then rip out the last row *stitch by stitch*. The important part is placing the live stitches back on the needle correctly. Here's how to do it.

To put stitches back onto the knitting needle, insert the tip of the needle into each one *from back to front*, making sure that the right "leg" of each stitch is to the front of the needle (see illustration 2).

Easy, right?

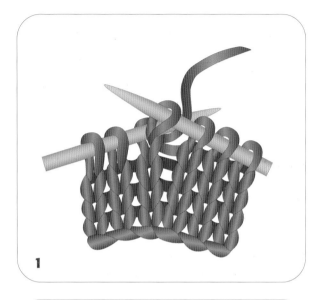

1

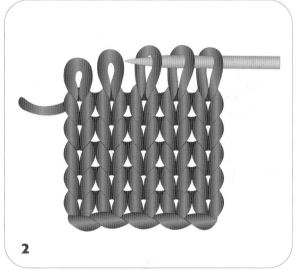

2

Reading Knitting Patterns

Okay, you've gathered together your tools and materials, you've learned all the basics of the craft, and you're ready to start your first project. But when you look at the pattern, you might feel overwhelmed, or worse, completely lost. Don't worry—it's not hard to navigate a pattern once you know how.

Patterns, such as those in this book, provide written instructions for creating knitted projects. They're usually comprised of several sections such as the following. It's always a good idea to read through the entire pattern before getting started so you'll know what to expect.

BASIC ELEMENTS

This section shows you how to interpret the various sections of a knitting pattern. A pattern isn't hard to read once you learn how!

Skill Level

This heading indicates the technical difficulty of the project. If you're a beginner, you'll probably want to start with Level 1, but be sure to progress through more

advanced patterns as you become more experienced. You'll learn more by challenging yourself—and trust me, you'll enjoy the process!

Sizes

This section lists the sizes for which the pattern is written. Parentheses separate the larger sizes from the smaller ones. You might find it helpful to circle all pertinent numbers and measurements for your size before you begin knitting.

Finished Measurements

Here you'll find the measurements for all sizes of the project that are included in the pattern. These reflect the measurements after sewing the seams.

Materials

This section lists all tools and materials that are necessary to complete the project. In this book, yarn equivalency information is included to make yarn substitution simple.

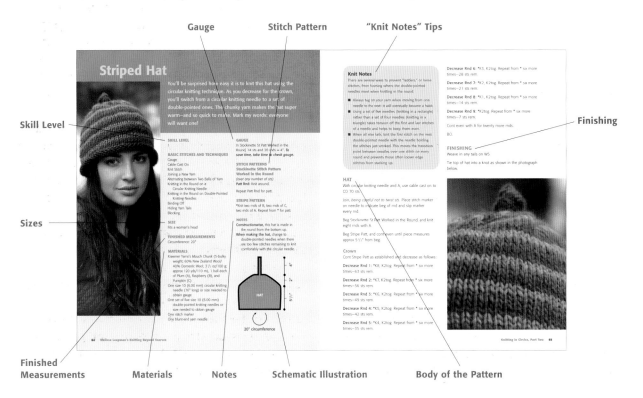

Gauge Stitch Pattern "Knit Notes" Tips

Skill Level

Sizes

Finished Measurements Materials Notes Schematic Illustration Body of the Pattern

Finishing

Gauge

Gauge refers to the number of stitches and rows per inch of knitted fabric, and it reflects the size of each individual stitch.

It's essential to understand gauge in order to be able to control the finished size of your knitted project. Several factors affect the size of stitches: thick yarns create larger stitches than finer ones; big, fat knitting needles produce larger stitches than smaller needles; metal needles often result in looser stitches than wooden ones. Even your mood can affect your gauge: knitting nervously during a scary movie will surely yield a tighter gauge than knitting while lying on a beach on vacation!

Commercial patterns, including those in this book, are written for a particular gauge. For your finished project to be the same size as the one listed in the pattern and match the one photographed, you must obtain the gauge called for. So be sure to measure your gauge correctly (and frequently!) as you work.

Often, patterns indicate the desired gauge over 4" rather than over 1". Since individual stitches tend to vary slightly in size, taking the average over a larger width yields a more accurate determination of the gauge of the fabric.

To measure your gauge accurately, knit a gauge swatch, bind off all stitches, then pin the fabric on a flat surface. Make sure that your piece of knitted fabric is at least 5" square: you'll want to avoid the edge stitches on all sides of the fabric, since these edge stitches tend to be ugly and wonky in size and are not representative of most of your fabric. Besides, they will mostly be hidden within the seams of your project and will not affect its finished measurements.

Without pressing down too hard—you don't want to compress the fabric or stretch out the stitches—count the number of stitches over 4", staying away from all edges of the fabric (see illustration above).

Divide that number by four to determine your stitch gauge. In our first example, there are 13 stitches over 4", making our gauge 3 1/4 stitches to the inch.

If you come up with partial stitches, do not simply ignore them! The difference of a half stitch per inch on a tiny piece of fabric will turn out to be much more dramatic over a larger one! If you see 22 stitches over 4", then your gauge is 5 1/2 stitches per inch. That half stitch counts!

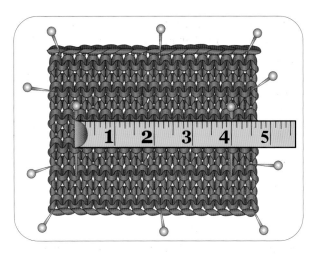

If you have fewer stitches per inch than what is specified in the pattern, switch to smaller knitting needles; if you have more stitches, switch to larger ones. Try changing one needle size to see if that makes a difference. Keep changing sizes until you obtain the gauge required. *When knitting, it doesn't matter what size knitting needles you use, only that your gauge matches the one called for in the pattern.* If necessary, knit up a new swatch with different-sized needles to test your gauge and remeasure. Sure, you're excited to begin knitting the actual project, but believe me, it is worth taking the time to obtain the correct gauge at the very beginning. It'll take only a few minutes of your time and will ensure that you'll be happy with your finished project.

Be sure to work your gauge swatch in the stitch pattern called for. Projects at the beginning of this book are worked in Garter Stitch Pattern; later ones include other textures, including Stockinette Stitch Pattern and various ribbings. Measure the gauge for these fabrics in the same manner.

As you knit your project pieces, recheck your gauge frequently, as it tends to change. As your gauge changes, switch to a different needle size to compensate.

The row gauge is often less crucial than the stitch gauge, because patterns usually tell you to stop knitting or to add shaping once a certain measurement is reached (rather than after a particular row number). However, if instructed to measure your row gauge, do it the same way discussed above except count the number of rows rather than stitches.

Stitch Pattern

Each stitch pattern used to create the project is listed here. Some stitch patterns require a certain number of stitches in order for the stitches to line up correctly across a knitted row. In those cases, the multiple of stitches necessary is indicated in this section.

Notes

This section of the pattern points out special information that you'll need to know in order to complete your project successfully. Specific instructions about assembly, for example, are given here.

"Knit Notes" Tips

Just as I've done in this lesson, I've included "Knit Notes" tips throughout the pattern sections of this book to make your knitting easier and more fun. To make them quick to find, they're located in colored boxes.

Body of the Pattern

Most of every pattern consists of instructions to make various pieces of the project: the back, front, sleeves, etc. Look for separate sections for each pattern piece. Areas that are crucial to shaping (such as armhole shaping) are set off in separate paragraphs with bold headings.

Finishing

This section of the pattern details all the steps, in order, that are required to complete the project, including blocking, seaming, and any embellishments such as tassels or fringe. After spending the time knitting up your pieces, take the time to finish up these last steps of the project correctly. It'll be worth the effort!

Schematic Illustration

This drawing shows the pieces of the project flat and indicates all important measurements. It'll come in handy when deciding which size to knit and also while blocking.

THE KNITTING LANGUAGE

The terminology in written knitting patterns might appear like a foreign language when you first see it. Long, wordy instructions take up lots of space on the printed page and appear even more daunting than knitting shorthand. Be patient as you learn the new vocabulary.

As you progess through the following lessons (and knit your way through the projects) you'll come across other terms that might be unfamiliar. Here's what they mean.

- **Garter Stitch** Garter stitch fabric is the simplest stitch pattern to knit. Comprised only of basic knit stitches, it is reversible and completely noncurling.
- **Knitwise** If a pattern tells you to insert your needle knitwise, insert your right-hand knitting needle into the indicated stitch *from left to right* as if you're about to knit the stitch (see illustration on page 95).
- **Purlwise** If a pattern tells you to insert your needle purlwise, insert your right-hand knitting needle into the indicated stitch *from right to left* as if you're about to purl the stitch (see illustration on page 95).
- **Reverse Shaping** When knitting garments such as cardigans in which shaping is identical but reversed, instructions are often given for one piece only; shaping for the second piece is worked on the opposite side to match, creating a mirror image.
- **Ribbing** Ribbed fabrics are formed when knit and purl stitches are stacked on top of each other vertically, such as in K1 P1 Rib. To create these stitch patterns, alternate knit and purl stitches according to the written pattern all the way across every row.
- **Stockinette Stitch** One of the most common stitch patterns, stockinette stitch fabric is smooth on one side and bumpy on the other side. To knit it, just alternate one row of knit stitches with one row of purl stitches.
- **Working Even** When you see this phrase in a knitting pattern, it means to continue knitting (or purling) in the stitch pattern as set without increasing or decreasing stitches.

ABBREVIATIONS

Here's a list of abbreviations and typical knitting pattern conventions. You might want to mark this page or photocopy the list so it's handy whenever you need it for reference.

approx — approximately

beg — begin(ning)

BO — bind off

CO — cast on

cont — continu(e)(ing)

dec — decreas(e)(ing)

dpn(s) — double-pointed knitting needle(s)

g — gram(s)

inc — increas(e)(ing)

K — knit

K2tog (knit two together) — knit two stitches together in their front loops as one stitch

K3tog (knit three together) — knit three stitches together in their front loops as one stitch

LH — left-hand

M1 (make one) — insert the left-hand needle under the horizontal strand between two stitches *from front to back*, and knit the picked-up strand *through the back loop*

mm — millimeter(s)

mult — multiple(s)

oz — ounce(s)

P — purl

P2tog (purl two together) — purl two stitches together in their front loops as one stitch

P3tog (purl three together) — purl three stitches together in their front loops as one stitch

patt(s) — pattern(s)

rem — remain(ing)

rep — repeat

RH — right-hand

rnd(s) — round(s)

RS — right side of fabric; the side that's typically visible during normal use; also called public side

SSK (slip, slip, knit) — slip the first and second stitches *one at a time knitwise* from the left-hand needle to the right-hand needle, then insert the tip of the left-hand needle into the fronts of these stitches and knit them together from this position

SSP (slip, slip, purl) — slip the first and second stitches *one at a time knitwise* from the left-hand needle to the right-hand needle, then slip them back to the left-hand needle; insert the tip of the right-hand needle *through the back loops* of the two stitches (going into the second stitch first), and purl them together as one stitch

SSSK (slip, slip, slip, knit) — slip the first, second, and third stitches *one at a time knitwise* from the left-hand needle to the right-hand needle, then insert the tip of the left-hand needle into the fronts of these stitches and knit them together from this position

SSSP (slip, slip, slip, purl) — slip the first, second, and third stitches *one at a time knitwise* from the left-hand needle to the right-hand needle, then slip them back to the left-hand needle; insert the tip of the right-hand needle *through the back loops* of the three stitches (going into the third stitch first), and purl them together as one stitch

st(s) — stitch(es)

tog — together

WS — wrong side of fabric; the side that's not typically visible during normal use

yd — yard(s)

* — repeat the instructions after the asterisk or between asterisks across the row or for as many times as instructed

( ) — repeat the instructions within the parentheses as many times as instructed

[ ] — repeat the instructions within the brackets as many times as instructed

Garter Stitch Hat

Now that you know how to cast on and knit a solid garter stitch piece of fabric, you can easily make this cute hat. Just knit a rectangle, bind off, sew the cast-on and bind-off edges together, and then gather up the top to form the crown! What could be simpler?

SKILL LEVEL
1

BASIC STITCHES AND TECHNIQUES
Gauge
Cable Cast On
Knit Stitch
Binding Off
Hiding Yarn Tails
Blocking
Whipstitch Seam

SIZES
Adult Small/Medium (Medium/Large). *Instructions are for smaller size, with changes for other size noted in parentheses as necessary.*

FINISHED MEASUREMENTS
Circumference: 18 (21)"
Length (before turning up cuff):
　　10 (11)"

MATERIALS
Plymouth Yarn Company's *Outback Wool* (4-worsted weight; 100% wool; 7 oz/200 g; approx 370 yds/338 m), 1 hank of Plum Variegated #959
One pair of size 8 (5.00 mm) knitting needles or size needed to obtain gauge
One blunt-end yarn needle

GAUGE
In Garter St Patt, 16 sts and 32 rows = 4". *To save time, take time to check gauge.*

STITCH PATTERN
Garter Stitch Pattern
(over any number of sts)
Patt Row: Knit across.

Repeat Patt Row.

Knit Notes
Always begin and end every piece of knitting with an extra-long yarn tail. If you use them to sew up your seams, you'll have fewer ends to hide!

HAT

18 (21)"

10 (11)"

HAT

Use cable cast on to CO 40 (44) sts.

Beg Garter St Patt, and cont even until piece measures approx 18 (21)" from beg.

BO, leaving an 8" tail.

FINISHING

Weave in any yarn tails on WS *except those to be used later in seaming the edge and gathering the crown*.

Block to measurements.

Use whipstitch to sew the cast-on edge of the rectangle to its bind-off edge.

Weave yarn tail through sides of rows and pull yarn tautly, gathering top of hat. Secure by making a tiny knot, and weave in tail to WS.

Fold up 2" at lower edge for cuff.

adding more yarn

When knitting larger projects, you'll have to attach additional yarn when the first ball is used up. This lesson tells you how to do it.

Joining a New Yarn

To attach new yarn, leave a 6" tail and drop the old yarn. Then grab the new yarn, leave a 6" tail, and knit the next stitch with the new yarn (see illustration 1). You'll weave in these yarn ends later.

If you must attach a new ball of yarn in the middle of a row, don't worry; simply drop the old yarn, then use the new one to knit the next stitch (see illustration 2). Begin and end with 6" tails and continue knitting.

If those loose, dangling bits of yarn distract you as you knit, don't just cut them off! Instead, make temporary square knots to secure them (see illustration 3). Later, use a pointed-end yarn needle to weave them in. (If you don't remember how to do this, refer back to "Weaving in Yarn Tails to Hide Them" on page 18.)

Knit Notes

To make the joining of yarn as invisible as possible, try to attach the new strand at the beginning of a row whenever you can. If you're coming toward the end of your ball of yarn and you're at the end of a row, just stop short and attach a new ball. Your woven-in yarn tails will be harder to see if they're near the side edge of your project.

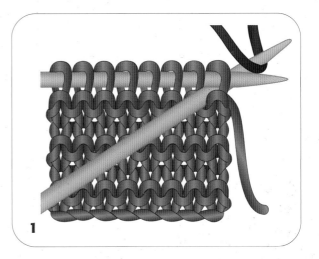

1

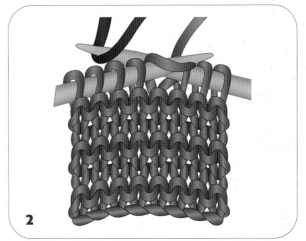

2

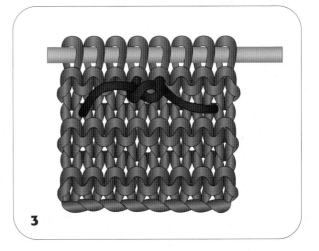

3

Wrap

Just knit two oversized rectangular-shaped pieces and sew them together to create this dramatic piece!

SKILL LEVEL
1

BASIC STITCHES AND TECHNIQUES
Gauge
Cable Cast On
Knit Stitch
Joining a New Yarn
Binding Off
Hiding Yarn Tails
Blocking
Whipstitch Seam

SIZE
One size

FINISHED MEASUREMENTS
19 × 53"

MATERIALS
Unique Kolours/Colinette's *Tagliatelli* (5-bulky weight; 90% merino wool/10% nylon; 3 1/2 oz/100 g; approx 159 yds/145 m), 6 hanks of Fire #71
One size 13 (9.00 mm) circular knitting needle (29" or longer) or size needed to obtain gauge
One blunt-end yarn needle

GAUGE
In Garter St Patt, 9 sts and 20 rows = 4".
To save time, take time to check gauge.

STITCH PATTERN
Garter Stitch Pattern
(over any number of sts)
Patt Row: Knit across.

Repeat Patt Row.

Knit Notes
Often, when a large number of stitches are to be worked per row as for the rectangles in this project, regular straight knitting needles aren't long enough to accommodate all of them. In these instances, use circular needles. Just work back and forth in rows as you would normally and ignore the cable that connects the needle points!

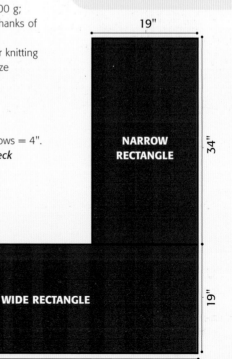

19"

NARROW RECTANGLE

34"

19"

WIDE RECTANGLE

53"

WIDE RECTANGLE

Use cable cast on to CO 119 sts.

Beg Garter St Patt, and cont even until piece measures approx 19" from beg, ending after WS row.

BO.

NARROW RECTANGLE

Use cable cast on to CO 77 sts.

Beg Garter St Patt, and cont even until piece measures approx 19" from beg, ending after WS row.

BO.

FINISHING

Weave in any tails on WS, *except those to be used later in seaming*.

Block pieces to measurements.

Position pieces according to schematic illustration on page 30 and use whipstitch to sew the pieces tog.

Weave in any remaining yarn tails to WS.

working with fringe

Fringe is fun to make and adds a decorative touch to a knitted item. This section shows you how.

Making and Attaching Fringe

Fringe is a pretty embellishment—and more! It can also stabilize the edge of a piece of knitted fabric, making it less likely to curl. Here's how to make it.

1 Cut a piece of cardboard to a length slightly longer than the desired length of your fringe.

2 Wind the yarn loosely around the cardboard the number of times specified in the pattern. Then cut the wrapped yarn along one edge, grasping the yarn with one hand to keep it all together.

3 With the right side of your knitted fabric facing you, fold the strands of yarn in half and then use a crochet hook to loop the folded strands onto the edge of the knitted piece, pulling the loop to the wrong side of the fabric.

4 To secure the fringe, pull the loose ends of yarn through the folded loop and tighten (see the illustration below).

5 For a neat finish, trim the fringe evenly.

Fringed Shoulder Bag

It takes only three rectangular-shaped pieces to make this cool bag! As you learned from this lesson, the fringe is easy to add, and it's perfect for showing off the special suede-like yarn.

SKILL LEVEL
1

BASIC STITCHES AND TECHNIQUES
Gauge
Cable Cast On
Knit Stitch
Joining a New Yarn
Binding Off
Whipstitch Seam
Hiding Yarn Tails
Blocking
Making and Attaching Fringe

SIZE
One size

FINISHED MEASUREMENTS
10$\frac{1}{4}$ × 8"

MATERIALS
Berroco's *Suede Tri-Color* (4-worsted weight; 100% nylon; 1$\frac{3}{4}$ oz/50 g; approx 120 yds/110 m), 3 balls of Buffalo Bill #3793 (A)
Berroco's *Suede* (4-worsted weight; 100% nylon; 1$\frac{3}{4}$ oz/50 g; approx 120 yds/110 m), 2 balls of Tonto #3715 (B)
One pair *each* of sizes 6 and 7 (4.00 and 4.50 mm) knitting needles or size needed to obtain gauge
One blunt-end yarn needle
One size F/5 (3.75mm) crochet hook (for attaching fringe)
[Optional: coordinating fabric for lining]
[Optional: sewing thread to match fabric]
[Optional: plastic canvas for added stability]
[Optional: one sharp-end sewing needle]

GAUGE
With larger needles in Garter St Patt, 20 sts and 40 rows = 4". *To save time, take time to check gauge.*

STITCH PATTERN
Garter Stitch Pattern
(over any number of sts)
Patt Row: Knit across.

Repeat Patt Row.

Knit Notes
It's a good, practical idea to line a knitted bag. This keeps jagged-edged objects such as keys from catching on stitches and pointy-tipped pens from poking through the fabric. To make your bag even sturdier, slip a piece of plastic canvas (widely available at crafts stores) under the lining—you'll be able to carry all your daytime stuff without worry!

BACK

With larger needles and A, use cable cast on to CO 52 sts.

Beg Garter St Patt, and cont even until piece measures approx 17 1/2" from beg.

BO.

FRONT

Same as back until piece measures approx 8" from beg.

BO.

STRAP/GUSSET

With smaller needles and B, use cable cast on to CO 11 sts.

Beg Garter St Patt, and cont even until strap measures approx 67" from beg.

BO.

FINISHING

Weave in any tails on WS, *except those to be used later in seaming*.

Block pieces to measurements.

Whipstitch cast-on edge of strap/gusset to its bind-off edge.

Centering strap/gusset seam at center bottom of front, whipstitch one side of strap/gusset to front.

Whipstitch other side of strap/gusset to back, leaving 9 1/2" unsewn for top flap.

Weave in any remaining yarn tails to WS.

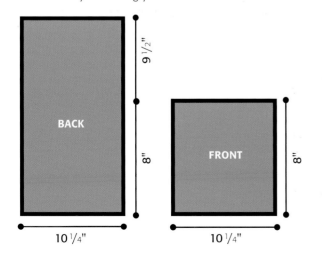

Fringe

Cut fifty-two 16" lengths of A.

With RS facing and using crochet hook, attach two lengths of fringe in every other stitch along edge of top flap.

Trim fringe evenly.

[Optional: Cut fabric to match front, back (including flap), and gusset portion of strap, adding 1/4" selvage on all sides. Sew pieces together to form lining. Cut plastic canvas to match size of interior portion of bag and secure to inside. Sew lining into place, folding 1/4" to WS on all sides (plastic canvas is sandwiched in between knitted fabric and lining).]

juggling two balls of yarn

Occasionally you'll want to add contrasting colored stripes to your knitting. Working horizontal stripes is quite easy, as you'll see in this lesson.

Alternating between Two Balls of Yarn

When working narrow horizontal stripes, it isn't necessary to cut the yarn after each color (and create oodles of yarn tails that then have to be woven in). If each stripe consists of an *even* number of rows, you can carry the unused yarn *loosely* up the side of the fabric until it is used again. By using this technique, you'll find that finishing your project will be faster and easier.

To do this, drop the first color and grab the new one from underneath the old one, and continue knitting (see the illustration below).

Be sure not to pull on the new yarn too tightly or else your fabric will pucker at the side edge!

After you've knitted an even number of rows with the new color and it's time to return to the old one, it'll be waiting there on the correct side of the fabric for you to pick up and knit with! Just grab it from underneath the one you've been using and keep knitting.

Knit Notes

Sometimes this same technique is used when knitting with variegated or hand-dyed yarn (see the "Ribbed Cami" on page 115, for example). Alternating between two balls of yarn every couple of rows creates invisible "stripes" that prevent "pools," or blotches, of color. Alternating this way also evens out the inevitable variations found within a single dye lot of a hand-painted yarn.

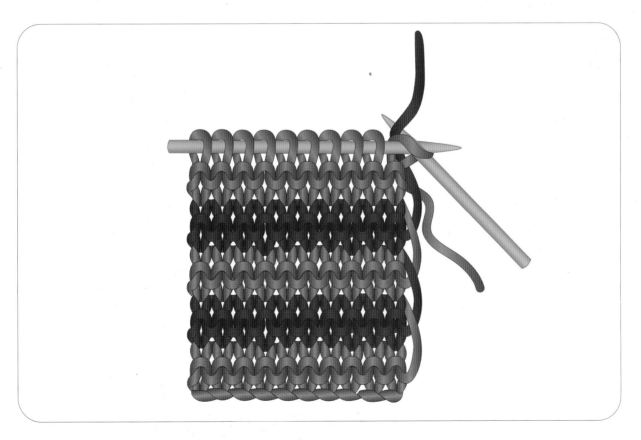

Poncho

This poncho is comprised of two rectangles sewn together. Sure, it'll take a little longer to knit than a scarf, but it'll be that much warmer! While knitting it, you'll practice making narrow horizontal stripes.

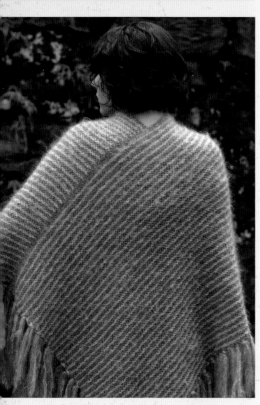

SKILL LEVEL
1

BASIC STITCHES AND TECHNIQUES
Gauge
Cable Cast On
Knit Stitch
Joining a New Yarn
Alternating between Two Balls of Yarn
Binding Off
Hiding Yarn Tails
Blocking
Whipstitch Seam
Making and Attaching Fringe

SIZES
Small (Medium, Large). *Instructions are for smallest size, with changes for other sizes noted in parentheses as necessary.*

FINISHED MEASUREMENTS
Length (from shoulder to lowest point):
Approx 29 (32, 35)"

MATERIALS
Classic Elite's *La Gran* (5-bulky weight; 76.5% mohair/17.5% wool/ 6% nylon; 1 1/2 oz/42 g; approx 90 yds/82 m), 7 balls *each* of Dark Denim #6592 (A) and Light Denim #6595 (B)
One size 9 (5.50 mm) circular knitting needle (29" or longer) or size needed to obtain gauge
One size H/8 (5.00 mm) crochet hook (for attaching fringe)
One blunt-end yarn needle

GAUGE
In Garter St Stripe Patt, 17 sts and 28 rows = 4". *To save time, take time to check gauge.*

STITCH PATTERN
Garter Stitch Stripe Pattern
(over any number of sts)
Rows 1 and 2: Knit across with A.

Rows 3 and 4: Knit across with B.

Repeat Rows 1–4 for patt.

NOTES
When knitting the rectangles, Rows 1 and 3 are RS rows.
For ease in finishing, do not cut yarn at end of stripes; rather, carry it *loosely* up side of work on WS.
When knitting, use a circular knitting needle in order to accommodate the large number of stitches.

Knit Notes
For a totally different look, choose one variegated and one solid color yarn. Just make sure the laundering instructions and knitting gauge match those of the original yarns!

RECTANGLE

(Make two)

With A, use cable cast on to CO 111 (119, 130) sts.

Beg Garter St Stripe Patt, and cont even until piece measures approx 18½ (20½, 23)" from beg, ending after Row 2.

BO.

FINISHING

Weave in any tails on WS, *except those to be used later in seaming*.

Block pieces to measurements.

With RS facing, whipstitch rectangles tog, following the illustration below.

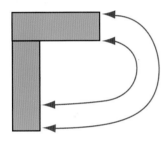

Weave in any remaining yarn tails to WS.

Fringe

For each tuft of fringe, cut two 12" lengths *each* of A and B.

With RS facing, using crochet hook and holding two strands *each* of A and B, attach fringe evenly spaced along lower edge of poncho as desired.

Trim fringe evenly.

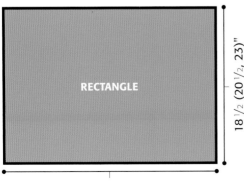

RECTANGLE

18½ (20½, 23)"

26 (28, 30½)"

Sideways Striped Shell

The vertical stripes in this little top make it especially flattering. No one will ever guess how easy it was to knit! For super-quick finishing, don't cut the yarn after each stripe. Instead, carry it *loosely* up the side of the fabric until you need it again.

SKILL LEVEL
1

BASIC STITCHES AND TECHNIQUES
Gauge
Cable Cast On
Knit Stitch
Joining a New Yarn
Alternating between Two Balls of Yarn
Binding Off
Hiding Yarn Tails
Blocking
Whipstitch Seam

SIZES
Small (Medium, Large, 1X, 2X, 3X).
Instructions are for smallest size, with changes for other sizes noted in parentheses as necessary.

FINISHED MEASUREMENTS
Bust: 32 (36, 38, 40, 44, 46)"
Length: 18 (18, 18¾, 19¼, 19¾, 19¾)"

MATERIALS
JCA/Reynolds Yarn's *Blossom* (5-bulky weight; 50% acrylic/40% viscose/ 10% cotton; each approx 1¾ oz/ 50 g and 82 yd/75 m), 4 (5, 5, 6, 6, 7) balls *each* of Periwinkle Blue #24 (A) and Sky Blue #6 (B)
One pair of size 7 (4.50 mm) knitting needles or size needed to obtain gauge
One blunt-end yarn needle

GAUGE
In Garter St Stripe Patt, 16 sts and 32 rows = 4". *To save time, take time to check gauge.*

STITCH PATTERN
Garter Stitch Stripe Pattern
(over any number of sts)
Rows 1 and 2: Knit across with A.

Rows 3 and 4: Knit across with B.

Repeat Rows 1–4 for patt.

NOTES
Constructionwise, this sweater is made sideways.
For ease in finishing, do not cut yarn at end of stripes; rather, carry it *loosely* up side of work on WS.

Knit Notes
Since this sweater is made sideways, *it is crucial to match the row gauge as well as the stitch gauge* called for in the pattern in order to achieve the size desired. To measure your gauge: cast on 24 stitches, knit 6" of Garter Stitch Stripe Pattern, and bind off. Then carefully count the number of stitches and rows over 4" in the center of your swatch. If you have *too many* stitches and rows, then your gauge is too tight; you'll have to *go up* one or two knitting needle sizes. *Too few* stitches and rows, on the other hand, indicate that your gauge is too loose; you'll have to *go down* one or two knitting needle sizes.

BACK

With A, use cable cast on to CO 47 (47, 48, 49, 49, 49) sts.

Beg Garter St Stripe Patt and cont even for 9 (17, 21, 25, 29, 33) rows.

Shape Armhole

With A, use cable cast on to CO 25 (25, 27, 28, 30, 30) sts at beg of row, then knit them as well as the original 47 (47, 48, 49, 49, 49) sts to end row—72 (72, 75, 77, 79, 79) sts.

Cont even in patt as established for 27 (27, 27, 27, 31, 31) more rows.

Shape Neck

Next Row (WS Row): With A, BO 6 sts at beg of row, then knit across to end row—66 (66, 69, 71, 73, 73) sts rem.

Cont even in patt as established for 55 more rows.

With A, use cable cast on to CO 6 sts at beg of row, then knit them as well as the original 66 (66, 69, 71, 73, 73) sts to end row—72 (72, 75, 77, 79, 79) sts.

Cont even in patt as established for 27 (27, 27, 27, 31, 31) more rows.

Shape Armhole

Next Row (WS): With A, BO 25 (25, 27, 28, 30, 30) sts at beg of row, then knit across to end row—47 (47, 48, 49, 49, 49) sts rem.

Cont even for 7 (15, 19, 23, 27, 31) rows.

Next Row (WS): With A, knit and BO.

FRONT

With A, use cable cast on to CO 47 (47, 48, 49, 49, 49) sts.

Beg Garter St Stripe Patt, and cont even for 9 (17, 21, 25, 29, 33) rows.

Shape Armhole

With A, use cable cast on to CO 25 (25, 27, 28, 30, 30) sts at beg of row, then knit them as well as the original 47 (47, 48, 49, 49, 49) sts to end row—72 (72, 75, 77, 79, 79) sts.

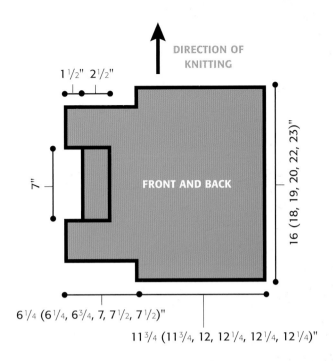

DIRECTION OF KNITTING

1 1/2" 2 1/2"

7"

FRONT AND BACK

16 (18, 19, 20, 22, 23)"

6 1/4 (6 1/4, 6 3/4, 7, 7 1/2, 7 1/2)"

11 3/4 (11 3/4, 12, 12 1/4, 12 1/4, 12 1/4)"

Cont even in patt as established for 27 (27, 27, 27, 31, 31) more rows.

Shape Neck

Next Row (WS Row): With A, BO 16 sts at beg of row, then knit across to end row—56 (56, 59, 61, 63, 63) sts rem.

Cont even in patt as established for 55 more rows.

With A, use cable cast on to CO 16 sts at beg of row, then knit them as well as the original 56 (56, 59, 61, 63, 63) sts to end row—72 (72, 75, 77, 79, 79) sts.

Complete same as back.

FINISHING

Weave in any tails on WS, *except those to be used later in seaming*.

Block pieces to measurements.

Use whipstitch to sew shoulder seams.

Use whipstitch to sew side seams.

Weave in any remaining yarn tails to WS.

knit stitch decreases, part one

What do you do when the pattern instructions call for decreasing the number of knit stitches in a row? This lesson introduces you to two kinds of knit stitch decreases.

Right-Slanting Knit Stitch Decreases

The simplest way to decrease stitches is simply to knit two stitches together. With this maneuver, the resulting stitch slants toward the right.

KNIT TWO TOGETHER DECREASE

When a pattern tells you to decrease one stitch by knitting two stitches together, do the following. With the working yarn in the back, insert the tip of the right-hand knitting needle into the first two stitches on the left-hand needle *knitwise from front to back*, as if they were a single stitch. Wrap the yarn around the right-hand needle as you would for a knit stitch, pull the yarn through both stitches, and knit a stitch, slipping both stitches off the left-hand needle at once (see illustration 1).

See? You've decreased one stitch, and the resulting stitch slants toward the right.

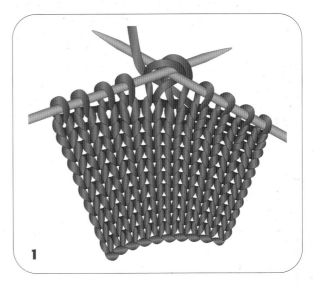

KNIT THREE TOGETHER DECREASE

To decrease two stitches at once, with the working yarn in the back, insert the tip of the right-hand knitting needle into *three* stitches on the left-hand needle *knitwise from front to back*, as if they were a single stitch. Wrap the yarn around the right-hand needle as you would for a knit stitch, pull the yarn through all three stitches, and knit a stitch, slipping all three stitches off the left-hand needle at once (see illustration 2).

Here, two stitches have been decreased, and the resulting stitch slants toward the right.

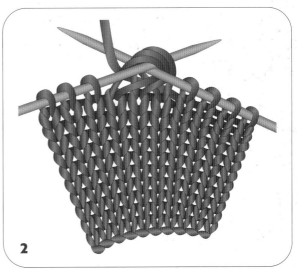

Knit Notes

Knitters have several ways to decrease the number of stitches in knitted fabrics. Why do you need to become familiar with several of them? Because each looks slightly different when knitted. When making sweaters, for example, you'll want to be able to work mirrored decreases on each side of the neck opening, having the stitches on one side slant to the right with stitches on the other side slanting to the left. In this lesson you learn knit stitch decreases that slant toward the right. In Lesson 10 on page 72, you'll find out how to make left-slanting knit stitch decreases.

Little Envelope Bag

Now that you know how to decrease, whip up a little rectangle, taper the top, and fold it up to create an adorable envelope to hold your spare coins or other treasures.

SKILL LEVEL
1

BASIC STITCHES AND TECHNIQUES
Gauge
Cable Cast On
Knit Stitch
Knit Two Together Decrease
Binding Off
Hiding Yarn Tails
Blocking
Whipstitch Seam

SIZE
One size

FINISHED MEASUREMENTS
Approx 4" wide × 3" high

MATERIALS
Trendsetter Yarn's *Dune* (4-worsted weight; 41% mohair/30% acrylic/ 12% viscose/11% nylon/6% metal; 1³/₄ oz/50 g; approx 90 yds/82 m), 1 ball of Jeweled Red #91
One pair of size 9 (5.50 mm) knitting needles or size needed to obtain gauge
One 1" button (JHB International's *Agoya Fiesta*, Style #70766 was used on sample project)
One blunt-end yarn needle

GAUGE
In Garter St Patt, 16 sts and 32 rows = 4".
To save time, take time to check gauge.

STITCH PATTERN
Garter Stitch Pattern
(over any number of sts)
Patt Row: Knit across.

Repeat Patt Row.

Knit Notes
Would you rather knit a larger everyday shoulder bag? You can easily change the dimensions of this pattern! Just multiply your desired width by the number of stitches you're knitting per inch (your stitch gauge over 1" of fabric) and cast on that increased number of stitches. For the triangular flap, decrease stitches as you knit, keeping in mind that since more stitches will be decreases, the flap will be longer.

BODY

Use cable cast on to CO 17 sts.

Beg Garter St Patt, and cont even until piece measures approx 6" from beg, ending after WS row.

TOP FLAP

Next (Dec) Row: K2tog, then knit across to end row—16 sts rem.

Repeat Dec Row thirteen more times—3 sts rem.

BO, leaving a 6" tail.

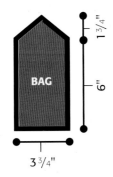

FINISHING

Fold yarn tail into shape of a loop to form a button loop that will fit around button; thread it through a blunt-end yarn needle; hold loop down with fingers; then sew it into position to secure it.

Weave in any tails on WS, *except those to be used later in seaming.*

Fold cast-on edge up 2³/₄", and use whipstitch to sew sides together.

Weave in any remaining yarn tails to WS.

Sew button onto front of bag opposite button loop.

Strap

Cut three 80" lengths of yarn.

Knot ends tog. Braid strands tog to create a 39" strap. Knot ends tog to secure the braid.

Use another piece of yarn to sew strap to inside of bag.

Weave in any remaining yarn tails to WS.

invisible (but oh-so-easy) seams, part one

When sewing the pieces of your project together, choose the method best suited to the task. Here you'll learn some new seaming methods.

Beautiful (I Mean Invisible) Seams on Garter Stitch Fabric

For virtually invisible seams in projects knitted in garter stitch fabric, use invisible weave seams. In garter stitch, this seaming technique is virtually invisible, lies flat, and adds no extra bulk. Later, in Lesson 14 on page 104, you'll learn other seaming methods for different types of stitch patterns.

VERTICAL-TO-VERTICAL INVISIBLE WEAVE SEAMS

This type of seam is useful for side seams of garments knitted in garter stitch.

1 To make this type of seam, lay the pieces of fabric flat, side by side, and with the right side of the fabric facing you, matching stripes, if applicable.

2 Thread a blunt-end yarn needle with the seaming yarn, leaving a 6" tail, and insert the needle into the bottom loop of the first horizontal ridge on one piece of fabric *from bottom to top*. Then go across and insert the needle into the top loop of the corresponding stitch on the other piece of fabric *also from bottom to top* (see illustration below).

3 Go back to the first piece of fabric and insert the needle into the bottom loop of the next horizontal ridge *from bottom to top*, then go back to the second piece of fabric and insert the needle into the top loop of the corresponding stitch *from bottom to top as before*.

4 Repeat these steps, joining each horizontal ridge, until the seam is completed. Cut the yarn, leaving a 6" tail.

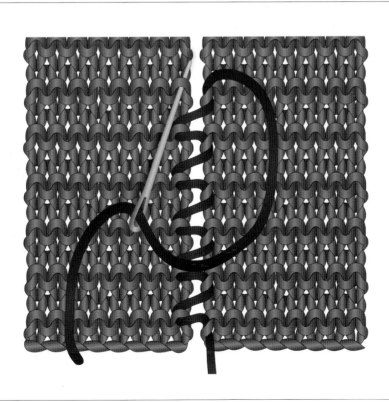

HORIZONTAL-TO-HORIZONTAL INVISIBLE WEAVE SEAMS

This type of seam is useful for shoulder seams of garments knitted in garter stitch when you're joining rows to rows.

1 To make this type of seam, lay the two pieces of fabric flat, with the right side of the fabric facing you, and place one piece on top of the other, with the bound-off edges together.

2 Thread a blunt-end yarn needle with the seaming yarn, leaving a 6" tail, and bring the needle up *from back to front* one-half stitch in on the right-hand edge of

the upper piece of fabric just above the bound-off edge and to the right of the first "V."

3 Bring the needle down *from front to back* into the center of the corresponding stitch in the lower piece of fabric just below the bound-off edge.

4 Still on the lower piece of fabric, bring the needle up *from back to front* through the center of the next stitch on the lower piece of fabric.

5 Go back to the upper piece of fabric, insert the needle down *into the same place it emerged before*, and bring it up to the left of the next stitch to the left.

6 Go back to the lower piece of fabric, insert the needle down *into the same place it emerged before*, and bring it up through the center of the next stitch to the left.

7 Repeat these steps until the seam is completed (see illustration below). Cut the yarn, leaving a 6" tail to be woven in later.

Knit Notes

As you're sewing this seam, notice that you're creating "V" stitches on the upper piece of fabric and upside-down "V" stitches on the lower piece of fabric. It'll help you keep track of your stitching!

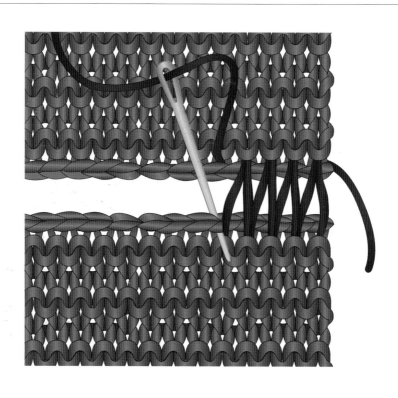

VERTICAL-TO-HORIZONTAL INVISIBLE WEAVE SEAMS

This type of seam is useful for setting in the sleeves of garments knitted in garter stitch.

1 To make this type of seam, lay the two pieces of fabric flat, with the right side of the fabric facing you, and place one piece on top of the other. The ridges (rows) of the upper piece should be horizontal, and the ridges of the lower piece should be vertical.

2 Thread a blunt-end yarn needle with the seaming yarn, leaving a 6" tail, and bring the needle up *from right to left* through the first ridge at the edge of the lower piece of fabric.

3 On the upper piece of fabric, insert the needle *from right to left* under both legs of the "V" of the first stitch just above the bound-off edge.

4 Go back to the lower piece of fabric and insert the needle *from right to left* through the next ridge of the fabric.

5 Go back to the upper piece of fabric, insert the needle down *into the same place it emerged before*, and bring it up just before the next stitch to the left. You should be going under both legs of the "V" of the stitch.

6 Repeat these steps until the seam is completed (see illustration below). Cut the yarn, leaving a 6" tail to be woven in later.

Knit Notes

As you're sewing this seam, notice how you're really just continuing the "V" stitches from the upper piece of fabric! That's what makes this type of seam so, well, seamless!

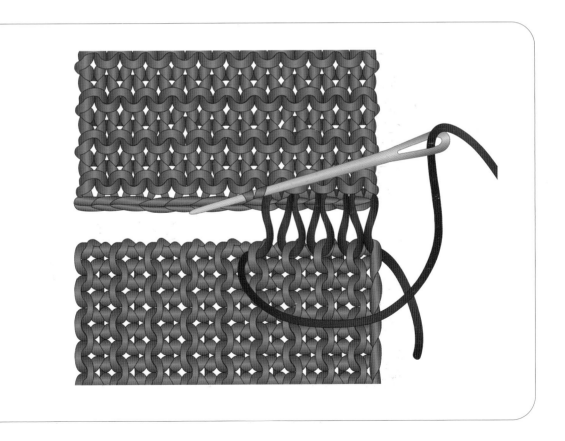

Bell Sleeve Pullover

Don't let the openwork pattern on these sleeves intimidate you! It is just a simple variation of garter stitch: every sixth row, instead of wrapping the yarn around the knitting needle once, wrap the yarn *three* times for every stitch. This maneuver creates extra-long and lacy stitches. Easy! During the final stages of this project, you'll practice invisible weave seams for a flawless finish.

SKILL LEVEL
1

BASIC STITCHES AND TECHNIQUES
Gauge
Cable Cast On
Knit Stitch
Joining a New Yarn
Knit Two Together Decrease
Binding Off
Hiding Yarn Tails
Blocking
Horizontal-to-Horizontal Invisible Weave
    Seam
Vertical-to-Horizontal Invisible Weave
    Seam
Vertical-to-Vertical Invisible Weave Seam

SIZES
Small (Medium, Large, 1X, 2X, 3X).
Instructions are for smallest size, with changes for other sizes noted in parentheses as necessary.

FINISHED MEASUREMENTS
Bust: 36 (40, 43, 47, 50½, 54)"
Length: 22½ (22¾, 23, 23½, 24, 24)"

MATERIALS
JCA/Artful Yarn's *Cinema* (4-worsted
    weight; 78% nylon/22% cotton; each
    approx 1¾ oz/50 g and 110 yd/
    101 m), 14 (15, 15, 16, 16, 17)
    balls of George Bailey #188
One pair of size 9 (5.50 mm) knitting
    needles or size needed to obtain
    gauge
One blunt-end yarn needle

GAUGE
In Garter St Patt, 22 sts and 40 rows =
4"; in Elongated Garter St Patt, 22 sts
and 22 rows = 4". *To save time, take
time to check gauge.*

STITCH PATTERNS
Garter Stitch Pattern
(over any number of sts)
Patt Row: Knit across.

Repeat Patt Row.
Elongated Garter Stitch Pattern
(over any number of sts)
See page 51 for stitch pattern.

NOTE
For sweater assembly, refer to the
    illustration for set-in construction on
    page 126.

Knit Notes
When working with ribbon yarn, don't worry about keeping it perfectly flat and untwisted as you knit. Instead, put the ball in a shoebox and place it a few yards away from you. By the time the yarn reaches your needles, it will relax and become easy to handle!

BACK

Use cable cast on to CO 99 (109, 119, 129, 139, 149) sts.

Beg Garter St Patt, and cont even until piece measures approx 15" from beg, ending after WS row.

Shape Armholes

BO 3 (3, 4, 4, 5, 5) sts at beg of next two rows—93 (103, 111, 121, 129, 139) sts rem.

Dec 1 st each side every row 1 (5, 7, 15, 15, 23) times, every other row 8 (10, 12, 8, 11, 7) times, then every fourth row 2 (0, 0, 0, 0, 0) times—71 (73, 73, 75, 77, 79) sts rem.

Cont even until piece measures approx 21 (21$\frac{1}{4}$, 21$\frac{1}{2}$, 22, 22$\frac{1}{2}$, 22$\frac{1}{2}$)" from beg, ending after WS row.

Shape Neck

Knit across first 11 (12, 12, 13, 14, 15) sts; join second ball of yarn and BO middle 49 sts, work to end of row.

Working both sides at once with separate balls of yarn, cont even until piece measures approx 22$\frac{1}{2}$ (22$\frac{3}{4}$, 23, 23$\frac{1}{2}$, 24, 24)" from beg, ending after WS row.

BO.

FRONT

Same as back.

SLEEVES

Use cable cast on to CO 85 (85, 91, 91, 95, 95) sts.

Beg Elongated Garter St Patt, and dec 1 st each side every eighth row 4 (0, 3, 0, 0, 0) times, every tenth row 5 (1, 3, 4, 4, 4) times, then every fourteenth row 0 (5, 2, 3, 3, 3) times—67 (73, 75, 77, 81, 81) sts rem.

Cont even in patt until piece measures approx 17$\frac{1}{2}$" from beg, ending after WS row.

Shape Cap

BO 3 (3, 4, 4, 5, 5) sts at beg of next two rows—61 (67, 67, 69, 71, 71) sts rem.

Dec 1 st each side every other row 1 (1, 1, 3, 3, 3) times, then every row 16 (19, 19, 18, 19, 19) times—27 sts rem.

BO 4 sts at beg of next four rows—11 sts rem.

BO.

FINISHING

Weave in any tails on WS, *except those to be used later in seaming*.

Block pieces to measurements.

Use horizontal-to-horizontal invisible weave seams to sew shoulder seams.

Elongated Garter Stitch Pattern

Row 1 (RS): Knit across.

Rows 2–4: As Row 1.

Row 5: Knit across, *wrapping yarn three times around needle* (see illustration 1).

Row 6: Knit across, *allowing extra loops to drop* (see illustration 2).

Repeat Rows 1–6 for patt.

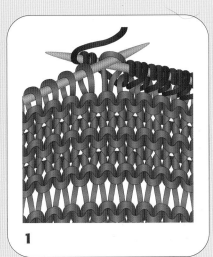
1

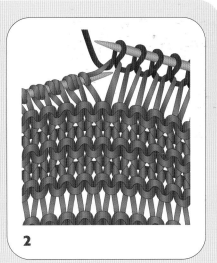
2

Use a combination of vertical-to-horizontal and vertical-to-vertical invisible weave seams to sew sleeves into the armholes.

Use vertical-to-vertical invisible weave seams to sew sleeve seams.

Use vertical-to-vertical invisible weave seams to sew side seams, leaving 3" open at lower edge for side slits.

Weave in any remaining yarn tails to WS.

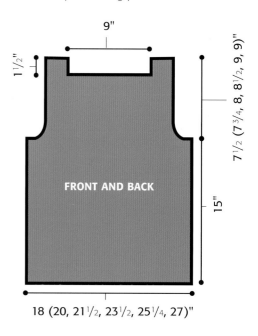

9"

1½"

7½ (7¾, 8, 8½, 9, 9)"

FRONT AND BACK

15"

18 (20, 21½, 23½, 25¼, 27)"

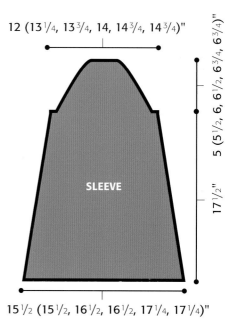

12 (13¼, 13¾, 14, 14¾, 14¾)"

5 (5½, 6, 6½, 6¾, 6¾)"

SLEEVE

17½"

15½ (15½, 16½, 16½, 17¼, 17¼)"

Cap Sleeve Pullover

By now you already have all the technical skills you need to knit this great off-the-shoulder top. In fact, I'll bet the hardest part of this project will be choosing which colors to use!

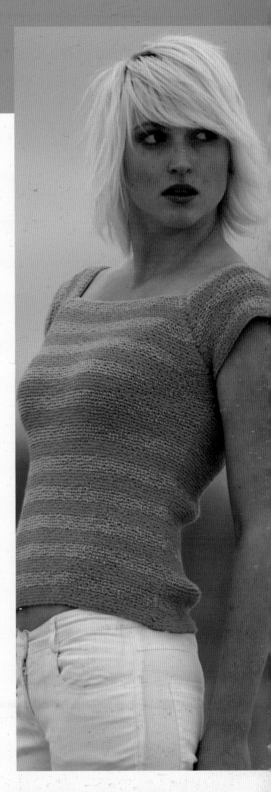

SKILL LEVEL
1

BASIC STITCHES AND TECHNIQUES
Gauge
Cable Cast On
Knit Stitch
Joining a New Yarn
Alternating between Two Balls of Yarn
Knit Two Together Decrease
Binding Off
Hiding Yarn Tails
Blocking
Vertical-to-Vertical Invisible Weave Seam

SIZES
Extra-Small (Small, Medium, Large, 1X, 2X). *Instructions are for smallest size, with changes for other sizes noted in parentheses as necessary.*

FINISHED MEASUREMENTS
Bust: 33 (36, 39, 42, 45, 48)"
Length: 18¼ (18¼, 18¾, 19¼, 19¾, 20¼)"

MATERIALS
Classic Elite's *Star* (3-DK weight; 99% cotton/1% cotton; each approx 1¾ oz/50 g and 112 yd/102 m), 5 (5, 6, 6, 7, 7) balls *each* of Mineral Water #5117 (A) and Lime Sherbet #5172 (B)
One pair of size 7 (4.50 mm) knitting needles or size needed to obtain gauge
One blunt-end yarn needle

GAUGE
In Garter St Stripe Patt, 22 sts and 44 rows = 4". *To save time, take time to check gauge.*

STITCH PATTERN
Garter Stitch Stripe Pattern
(over any number of sts)
Rows 1–10: Knit across with A.

Rows 11–20: Knit across with B.

Repeat Rows 1–20 for patt.

NOTES
For ease in finishing, do not cut yarn at end of stripes; rather, carry it *loosely* up side of work.
For Dec Row: K1, K2tog, knit across until 3 sts remain in row, ending row with K2tog, K1.
For sweater assembly, refer to the illustration for raglan construction on page 126.

Knit Notes
For a less sporty look, rather than all-over stripes, try knitting the first and last few rows of each sweater piece with a contrasting, faux-fur yarn with the rest of the sweater in a single color. *Très élégant!*

BACK

With A, use cable cast on to CO 91 (99, 107, 116, 124, 132) sts.

Beg Garter St Stripe Patt, and work even until piece measures approx 13¾" from beg, ending after Row 10.

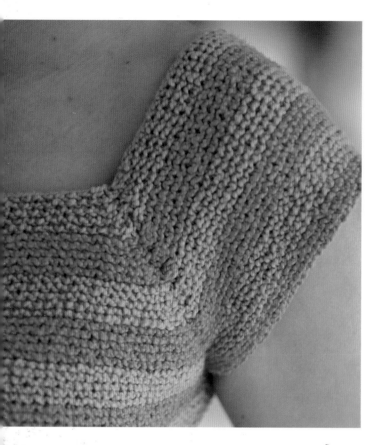

Shape Raglan

Cont in patt as established, and cont Dec Row (see Notes) every fourth row 3 (0, 0, 0, 0, 0) times, every other row 19 (24, 25, 27, 28, 29) times, then every row 0 (2, 5, 6, 9, 12) times—47 (47, 47, 50, 50, 50) sts rem.

BO.

FRONT

Same as back.

SLEEVES

With A, use cable cast on to CO 66 (66, 68, 72, 78, 78) sts.

Beg Garter St Stripe Patt with Row 16, *and at the same time,* work Dec Row (see Notes) every fourth row 10 (10, 11, 12, 11, 14) times, then every other row 5 (5, 5, 6, 10, 7) times—36 sts rem.

Cont even in patt for 0 (0, 1, 0, 1, 0) row(s).

BO.

FINISHING

Weave in any tails on WS, *except those to be used later in seaming.*

Block pieces to measurements.

Use vertical-to-vertical invisible weave seams to set in raglan sleeves, being careful to match stripes.

Use vertical-to-vertical invisible weave seams to sew side seams, being careful to match stripes.

Weave in any remaining yarn tails to WS.

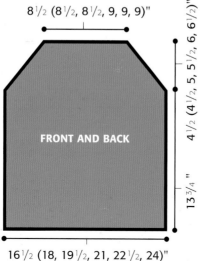

8½ (8½, 8½, 9, 9, 9)"

4½ (4½, 5, 5½, 6, 6½)"

FRONT AND BACK

13¾ "

16½ (18, 19½, 21, 22½, 24)"

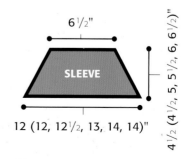

6½"

SLEEVE

4½ (4½, 5, 5½, 6, 6½)"

12 (12, 12½, 13, 14, 14)"

4½ (4½, 5, 5½, 6, 6½)"

knitting in circles, part one

Drop those straight needles and pick up a circular knitting needle, because this lesson shows you how to create tubular pieces of fabric without seams!

Knitting in the Round on a Circular Knitting Needle

So far you've been working back and forth in rows and knitting all of the stitches, creating ridged garter stitch fabric. Now you'll see how doing the exact same maneuver *in the round* on circular knitting needles (see "Needles" on page 12) creates a totally different effect—smooth stockinette stitch fabric!

To create tubular pieces of fabric without seams, you'll use the circular knitting technique.

1 To do this, use a circular knitting needle that's the length called for in the pattern, and cast on the required number of stitches.

Take the time to *ensure that the cast-on stitches are not twisted*. (If the stitches are twisted, the fabric that you create will also be twisted—and you'll have to start over!) You can prevent twisting by pointing the nubby edge of all of the cast-on stitches toward the center of the circle.

2 Hold the circular needle so that the last cast-on stitch is near the tip of the needle in your right hand and the first cast-on stitch is near the tip of the needle in your left hand. To join the stitches into a circle, knit the first stitch on the left-hand needle (the very first stitch you originally cast on) (see illustration below).

3 Continue knitting in this way around and around, *never turning the work*, until your knitted piece is the desired length.

When knitting in the round, the right side of the fabric is always facing you.

Knit Notes

It is helpful to slip a closed-ring marker (see "Other Knitting Tools" on page 12) onto the needle between the first and last stitches in order to indicate the beginning of a round of knitting. Use a uniquely colored marker here, especially if you're using other markers in the project to set off other pattern elements such as panels or shaping. It'll help you keep track of the number of rounds you've worked!

Tweed Skirt

You'll be amazed at how easy it is to make this great skirt! First, its lower borders are knitted back and forth in rows. The rest of the skirt is knitted in the round to the waistband on a circular knitting needle, decreasing as you go. Cool!

SKILL LEVEL
1

BASIC STITCHES AND TECHNIQUES
Gauge
Cable Cast On
Knitting in the Round on a
    Circular Needle
Knit Stitch
Joining a New Yarn
Knit Two Together Decrease
Binding Off
Whipstitch Seam
Hiding Yarn Tails
Blocking

SIZES
Small (Medium, Large). *Instructions are for smallest size, with changes for other sizes noted in parentheses as necessary.*

FINISHED MEASUREMENTS
Waist (before elastic is sewn in):
    29 (32, 35)"
Hip: 35 1/4 (40 1/2, 46 1/2)"
Length: 19"

MATERIALS
Classic Elite's *Beatrice* (4-worsted
    weight; 100% merino wool; each
    approx 1 3/4 oz/50 g and 63 yd/
    58 m), 8 (10, 12) balls of Mountain
    Meadow #3250 (A)
Classic Elite's *Bazic* (4-worsted weight;
    100% superwash wool; each approx
    1 3/4 oz/50 g and 65 yd/59 m),
    1 ball of Heliotrope #2947 (B)
One pair *each* of sizes 8 and 10 (5.00
    and 6.00 mm) knitting needles
Elastic, 3/4" wide, cut to fit waist

One stitch holder
One stitch marker
One safety pin
One blunt-end yarn needle
One piece of cardboard, approx 2 × 5"

GAUGE
With larger needles and A, in Stockinette St Patt Worked in the Round, 15 sts and 22 rnds = 4". *To save time, take time to check gauge.*

STITCH PATTERN
Stockinette Stitch Pattern Worked in the Round
(over any number of sts)
Patt Rnd: Knit around.

Repeat Patt Rnd for patt.

NOTE
Constructionwise, this garment is made from the bottom up.

Knit Notes
Would you prefer a longer (or shorter!) length for your skirt? No problem. Just add more rows (or work fewer, depending on your desired length) before the first Decrease Round and also between the first and second Decrease Rounds.

SKIRT

Lower Back Border

With smaller needles and A, use cable cast on to CO 72 (84, 96) sts.

Row 1 (RS): Knit across.

Rows 2–8: As Row 1.

Slip sts onto stitch holder.

Lower Front Border

Same as lower back border. After Row 8 is completed, do not slip sts onto holder.

Join Lower Borders to Form Side Slits

Using circular needle, knit across 72 (84, 96) sts from lower front border, then knit 72 (84, 96) sts from lower back border holder.

Join, *being careful not to twist sts*. Place stitch marker on needle to indicate beg of rnd and slip marker every rnd.

Cont even in Stockinette St Patt Worked in the Round on 144 (168, 192) sts until piece measures approx 6½" from beg.

Dec Rnd 1: *K10, K2tog. Repeat from * around— 132 (154, 176) sts rem.

Cont even in Stockinette St Patt Worked in the Round until piece measures approx 12½" from beg.

Dec Rnd 2: *K9, K2tog. Repeat from * around— 120 (140, 160) sts rem.

Cont even in Stockinette St Patt Worked in the Round until piece measures approx 18" from beg.

Dec Rnd 3: *K8, K2tog. Repeat from * around— 108 (126, 144) sts rem.

Put safety pin into fabric just below needle to mark beg of waistband.

Waistband

Cont even in Stockinette St Patt Worked in the Round until piece measures approx 20" from beg.

BO *loosely*.

FINISHING

Weave in any tails on WS.

Block to measurements.

Tie

Cut two strands of A, each approx 225" long.

Make a twisted cord approx 45" long as follows. Holding the two lengths together, fold them in half, and anchor one end to something stationary (such as a doorknob). Twist the strands clockwise about 100 times, and then fold in the middle, allowing the strands to twist back on themselves.

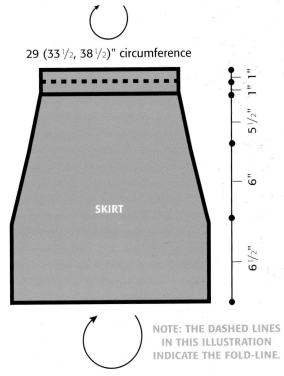

29 (33½, 38½)" circumference

1" 1" 5½" 6" 6½"

SKIRT

NOTE: THE DASHED LINES IN THIS ILLUSTRATION INDICATE THE FOLD-LINE.

38½ (45, 51)" circumference

Cut elastic to the desired waist length plus approx 1". Overlap the ends of elastic and sew them together. Fold the waistband in half to WS, and insert the elastic and twisted cord. Pull both ends of the twisted cord through the knitted fabric at center front.

Whipstitch waistband *loosely* into place.

Weave in any remaining yarn tails to WS.

With B, make two tassels (see "Knit Notes" for instructions) and attach one to each end of the tie.

Knit Notes

To make a tassel:

1 Cut a piece of cardboard to your desired tassel length.

2 Wind the yarn loosely around the cardboard several times; cut across one end.

3 Tightly tie a strand of yarn at the center of the tassel strands to attach them to the lower section of the twisted cord, and secure it with a square knot (see illustration 1).

4 Fold down the upper half of the tassel to cover the yarn used to attach the tassel strands to the twisted cord.

5 Use additional yarn to wrap the tassel strands approximately 1" from the top and fasten off (see illustration 2).

6 Trim the tassel evenly.

knitting in circles, part two

For knit projects with smaller circumferences, double-pointed knitting needles do the trick! You'll learn how to use them here.

Knitting in the Round on Double-Pointed Knitting Needles

Sometimes you may want to knit circular pieces with small circumferences, such as socks, the crowns of hats, and the lower edges of sleeves. Circular needles don't come in small enough lengths to knit these smaller circumferences comfortably, so for these types of projects, you can use a set of double-pointed knitting needles to get the job done.

It might look scary to knit with a handful of knitting needles at once. Sure, it's awkward at first, but once you get the hang of it you'll see how easy it is. Here's how:

1 To begin, use a circular knitting needle that's the same diameter as the double-pointed needles called for in the pattern and cast on the required number of stitches.

2 Then, on the first round of the switch, knit off approximately one-fourth of the total number of stitches from the circular needle onto each double-pointed needle (see illustration 1).

3 Form a square out of the four needles, positioning the working yarn at the upper right corner. To make certain that none of the stitches is twisted, place the nubby edge of all stitches on the cast-on edge toward the center of the square. (Remember, when working in the round, even a single twist in the first row will cause the entire piece of fabric to twist—and force you to start the whole project over!) Place a closed-ring marker (see "Other Knitting Tools" on page 12) on the needle to indicate the beginning of the round of knitting.

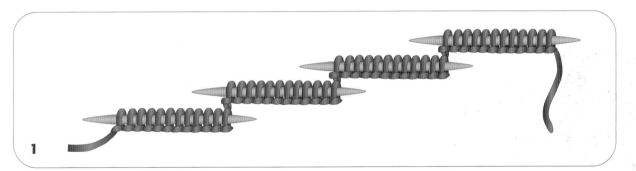

1

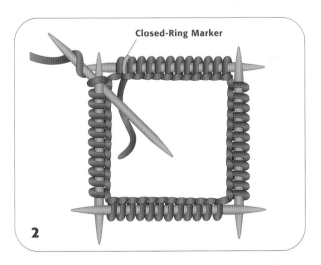

Closed-Ring Marker

2

4 Use the fifth double-pointed needle and knit across all the stitches on the first needle. Then use the needle you just emptied to knit across the stitches on the next needle (see illustration 2).

5 Repeat step 4 with each free needle, slipping the marker from the left-hand needle to the right-hand needle before starting each successive round.

Working with all these needles might look complicated, but you're knitting with only two needles at a time—just as you would with regular single-pointed needles!

Striped Hat

You'll be surprised how easy it is to knit this hat using the circular knitting technique. As you decrease for the crown, you'll switch from a circular knitting needle to a set of double-pointed ones. The chunky yarn makes the hat super warm—and so quick to make. Mark my words: everyone will want one!

SKILL LEVEL
1

BASIC STITCHES AND TECHNIQUES
Gauge
Cable Cast On
Knit Stitch
Joining a New Yarn
Alternating between Two Balls of Yarn
Knitting in the Round on a
    Circular Knitting Needle
Knitting in the Round on Double-Pointed
    Knitting Needles
Binding Off
Hiding Yarn Tails
Blocking

SIZE
Fits a woman's head

FINISHED MEASUREMENTS
Circumference: 20"

MATERIALS
Kraemer Yarns's *Mauch Chunk* (5-bulky
    weight; 60% New Zealand Wool/
    40% Domestic Wool; 3 1/2 oz/100 g;
    approx 120 yds/110 m), 1 ball *each*
    of Plum (A), Raspberry (B), and
    Pumpkin (C)
One size 10 (6.00 mm) circular knitting
    needle (16" long) or size needed to
    obtain gauge
One set of five size 10 (6.00 mm)
    double-pointed knitting needles or
    size needed to obtain gauge
One stitch marker
One blunt-end yarn needle

GAUGE
In Stockinette St Patt Worked in the
Round, 14 sts and 20 rnds = 4". *To
save time, take time to check gauge.*

STITCH PATTERNS
Stockinette Stitch Pattern
Worked in the Round
(over any number of sts)
Patt Rnd: Knit around.

Repeat Patt Rnd for patt.

STRIPE PATTERN
*Knit two rnds of B, two rnds of C,
two rnds of A. Repeat from * for patt.

NOTES
Constructionwise, this hat is made in
    the round from the bottom up.
When making the hat, change to
    double-pointed needles when there
    are too few stitches remaining to knit
    comfortably with the circular needle.

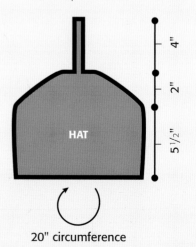

4"
2"
5 1/2"

HAT

20" circumference

HAT

With circular knitting needle and A, use cable cast on to CO 70 sts.

Join, *being careful not to twist sts*. Place stitch marker on needle to indicate beg of rnd and slip marker every rnd.

Beg Stockinette St Patt Worked in the Round, and knit eight rnds with A.

Beg Stripe Patt, and cont even until piece measures approx 5 1/2" from beg.

Crown

Cont Stripe Patt as established and decrease as follows:

Decrease Rnd 1: *K8, K2tog. Repeat from * six more times—63 sts rem.

Decrease Rnd 2: *K7, K2tog. Repeat from * six more times—56 sts rem.

Decrease Rnd 3: *K6, K2tog. Repeat from * six more times—49 sts rem.

Decrease Rnd 4: *K5, K2tog. Repeat from * six more times—42 sts rem.

Decrease Rnd 5: *K4, K2tog. Repeat from * six more times—35 sts rem.

Decrease Rnd 6: *K3, K2tog. Repeat from * six more times—28 sts rem.

Decrease Rnd 7: *K2, K2tog. Repeat from * six more times—21 sts rem.

Decrease Rnd 8: *K1, K2tog. Repeat from * six more times—14 sts rem.

Decrease Rnd 9: *K2tog. Repeat from * six more times—7 sts rem.

Cont even with A for twenty more rnds.

BO.

FINISHING

Weave in any tails on WS

Tie top of hat into a knot as shown in the photograph below.

a simple increase

Here you'll find out the simplest method of adding a stitch to your knitting—the Yarn Over Increase.

The Yarn Over Increase

This technique creates a hole in your fabric below where the increase is done. You've probably made lots of these unintentionally, but here's how it's officially done.

1 To do this kind of increase, bring the working yarn *between the knitting needles from back to front* (see illustration 1).

2 As you knit the next stitch off the left-hand needle, the yarn goes over the right-hand needle to create an extra stitch (see illustration 2). No other step is necessary.

The Yarn Over Increase comes in handy for making buttonholes, such as in the "Button-Up Bag" on page 68.

Knit Notes

If you'd like to make the increase totally invisible (such as when shaping the long sleeve of a sweater), knit the yarn over stitch you've created *through its back loop* on the following row to twist it. (For step-by-step instructions, see Lesson 11 on page 78.)

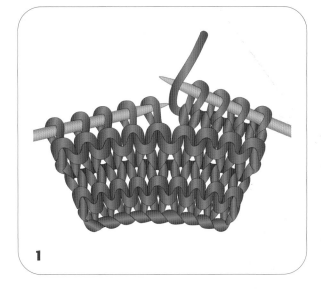

1

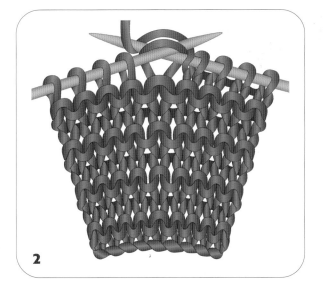

2

Button-Up Bag

This cute bag is always a favorite of students in my workshops. Only one row on each piece—the buttonhole row—requires concentration as yarn over increases are worked. The rest of the project is wonderfully familiar, rhythmic garter stitch.

SKILL LEVEL
1

BASIC STITCHES AND TECHNIQUES
Gauge
Cable Cast On
Knit Stitch
Yarn Over Increase
Joining a New Yarn
Binding Off
Hiding Yarn Tails
Blocking
Whipstitch Seam

SIZE
One size

FINISHED MEASUREMENTS
9¹⁄₂ × 6¹⁄₂"

MATERIALS
Classic Elite Yarn's *Paintbox* (5-bulky
    weight; 100% merino wool; 3¹⁄₂
    oz/100 g; approx 100 yds/91 m),
    2 balls of Windsor Violet #6832
One pair of size 11 (8.00 mm) knitting
    needles or size needed to obtain
    gauge
One blunt-end yarn needle
Two 5" square purse handles (Judi &
    Co's *Tortoise, Style #PL-10* was used
    on sample project)
Eight ⁷⁄₈" buttons (JHB International's
    Woods Hole, Style #50813 was used
    on sample project)
[Optional: coordinating fabric for lining]
[Optional: sewing thread to match fabric]
[Optional: one sharp-end sewing needle]

GAUGE
In Garter St Patt, 12 sts and 24 rows = 4".
To save time, take time to check gauge.

STITCH PATTERN
Garter Stitch Pattern
(over any number of sts)
Patt Row: Knit across.

Repeat Patt Row.

Knit Notes

Get more mileage out of a single set of purse handles: make lots of bags out of different novelty yarns (to suit your mood—and outfits) and just interchange the handles!

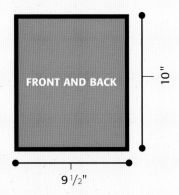

FRONT AND BACK

10"

9¹⁄₂"

BACK

Use cable cast on to CO 25 sts.

Beg Garter St Patt, and cont even for two rows.

Buttonhole Row

Next Row (RS): K2, yarn over, K7, yarn over, K7, yarn over, K7, yarn over, K2—29 sts.

Cont even in Garter St Patt until piece measures approx 10" from beg.

BO.

FRONT

Same as back.

FINISHING

Sew four buttons onto both front and back, approx 3 1/2" down from top, placing the first and last approx 1/4" from side edges and the other two evenly spaced between them.

Weave in any tails on WS, *except those to be used later in seaming.*

Use whipstitch to sew up sides and lower edge, leaving approx 3 1/2" unsewn at top.

Weave in any remaining yarn tails to WS.

Pull top of front through one handle, then fold the knitted fabric down and button handle into place. Repeat on other side for second handle.

[Optional: Cut fabric to match interior portion of front and back pieces, adding 1/4" selvage on all sides. Sew pieces together to form lining. Sew lining into place, folding 1/4" to WS on all sides.]

Sarong

Knit yourself this great beach cover-up. Worked in an easily memorized openwork pattern that'll give you tons of practice making yarn over increases, it's a breeze to knit!

SKILL LEVEL
2

BASIC STITCHES AND TECHNIQUES
Gauge
Cable Cast On
Knit Stitch
Knit Two Together Decrease
Yarn Over Increase
Joining a New Yarn
Binding Off
Hiding Yarn Tails
Blocking

SIZES
Small (Medium, Large, 1X). *Instructions are for smallest size, with changes for other sizes noted in parentheses as necessary.*

FINISHED MEASUREMENTS
Waist (wrapped): 27 (29, 31½, 34)"
Length: 27"

MATERIALS
Plymouth Yarn Company's *Bella Colour* (4-worsted weight; 55% cotton/45% acrylic; each approx 1¾ oz/50 g and 104 yd/95 m), 11 (12, 13, 14) balls of Sherbet #16

One size 10 (6.00 mm) circular knitting needle (29" long) or size needed to obtain gauge

GAUGE
In Faggoting Lace St Patt, 15 sts and 24 rows = 4". *To save time, take time to check gauge.*

STITCH PATTERN
Faggoting Lace Stitch Pattern
(over mult of 3 sts)
Patt Row: *K1, yarn over, K2tog. Repeat from * across.

Repeat Patt Row for patt.

NOTES
Constructionwise, this sarong is made from the bottom up.
When beginning this project, place a stitch marker on the first knitted row to indicate the right side of the fabric.

16"   13½ (14½, 15¾, 17)"   29½ (30½, 31½, 32½)"

3"

BODY

24"

41 (44, 47½, 50½)"

Knit Notes

Lacy fabrics, such as the one used to make this project, tend to be very malleable in shape. For accuracy when measuring this kind of fabric, lay your knitted piece flat on a smooth surface, being careful not to stretch it.

SKIRT

Use cable cast on to *loosely* CO 153 (165, 177, 189) sts.

Beg Faggoting Lace St Patt, and cont even until piece measures approx 24" from beg, ending after WS row.

Cast On for Ties

Use cable cast on to CO 60 sts at beg of next row—213 (225, 237, 249) sts.

Use cable cast on to CO 111 (114, 117, 120) sts at beg of next row—324 (339, 354, 369) sts.

Cont even in Faggoting Lace St Patt until tie measures approx $1/2$" from cast-on edge, ending after WS row.

Divide for Tie Slit

Next Row (RS): Beg with shorter tie, cont even in patt as established across first 111 (114, 120, 123) sts; join second ball of yarn, and cont even in patt as established to end row.

Work both sides at once with separate balls of yarn for approx 2", ending after WS row.

Break off second ball of yarn, leaving 6" tail.

Next Row (RS): Using the first ball of yarn only, cont even in patt as established across first 111 (114, 120, 123) sts, then join the top of slit and cont even in patt as established to end row.

Cont even in patt as established until tie measures approx 3" from cast-on edge.

BO *loosely*.

FINISHING

Weave in any tails on WS.

Block to measurements.

LESSON 10

knit stitch decreases, part two

You've learned all about right-slanting knit stitch decreases in Lesson 5 on page 42. Here's how to make some decreases that slant toward the left.

Left-Slanting Knit Stitch Decreases

Individual stitches are more noticeable in stockinette stitch fabric than the stitches done in garter stitch fabric—even decreases show up more in this smooth fabric. For beautiful finishing details, especially in sweaters and other garments, you'll want to be able to make decreases that slant to the left and also to the right. You've already mastered right-slanting knit stitch decreases in Lesson 5 on page 42. Now it's time to learn their mirror images!

SLIP, SLIP, KNIT DECREASE

To decrease one stitch while knitting and have the resulting stitch slant toward the left on the right side of the fabric, most knitters use the Slip, Slip, Knit Decrease.

1 To make this type of decrease, insert the tip of the right-hand needle *knitwise* into the first stitch on the left-hand needle and slip the stitch off onto the right-hand needle (see illustration 1).

2 Likewise, slip the next stitch *knitwise* from the left-hand needle onto the right-hand needle (see illustration 2). It's important that these stitches be slipped *one at a time*.

3 Now insert the tip of the left-hand needle into the *front* of both slipped stitches and knit them together from this position (see illustration 3).

One stitch has been decreased, and *the resulting stitch slants toward the left*. It is the mirror image of the Knit Two Together Decrease and is often paired with it in highly visible locations on garments, such as the shaping for raglan armholes or sleeve caps.

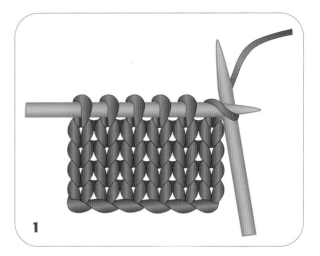

1

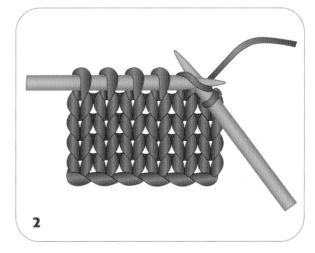

2

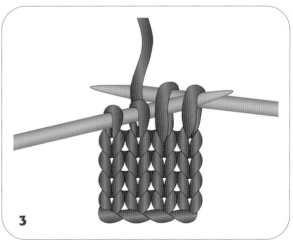

3

SLIP, SLIP, SLIP, KNIT DECREASE

To create a double-decrease (three stitches that become one stitch) that slants toward the left, make a Slip, Slip, Slip Knit Decrease. It's made the same way as an Slip, Slip, Knit Decrease but with one extra step: three stitches are slipped onto the right-hand needle instead of two.

1 To begin, insert the tip of the right-hand needle into the first stitch on the left-hand needle *knitwise* and then slip it off onto the right-hand needle (see illustration 1).

2 Slip the next stitch from the left-hand needle onto the right-hand needle *knitwise*. Be sure to slip these stitches *one at a time* (see illustration 2).

3 Repeat these steps for the next stitch on the left-hand needle—three stitches have been slipped knitwise from the left- to the right-hand knitting needle (see illustration 3). As with the Slip, Slip, Knit Decrease, it is crucial that these stitches each be slipped knitwise and *one at a time*.

4 Insert the tip of the left-hand needle into the front of all three slipped stitches at once and knit them together from this position (see illustration 4).

Voilà! Two stitches have been decreased, and the resulting stitch slants toward the left. Since it's the mirror image of a Knit Three Together Decrease, these two kinds of double-decreases are often worked in pairs, such as in sleeve caps and raglan armholes.

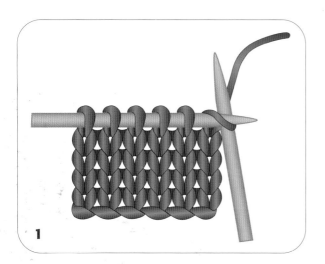

1

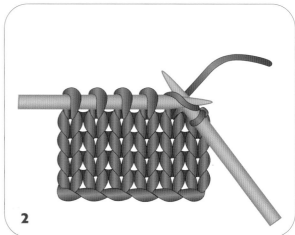

2

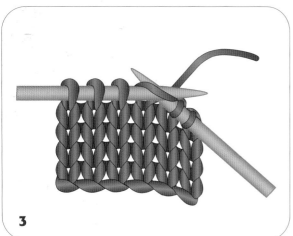

3

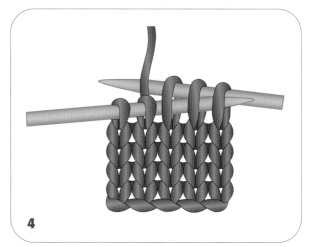

4

A-Line Skirt

Made in the round with symmetrical Slip, Slip, Knit and Knit Two Together Decreases, this funky skirt features picot hems at its edges. Once you try this fun technique, you'll find lots of places to use it, including the borders of hats, sweaters, and other projects.

SKILL LEVEL
2

BASIC STITCHES AND TECHNIQUES
Gauge
Cable Cast On
Knitting in the Round on a
    Circular Knitting Needle
Knit Stitch
Joining a New Yarn
Yarn Over Increase
Knit Two Together Decrease
Slip, Slip, Knit Decrease
Binding Off
Hiding Yarn Tails
Whipstitch Seam

SIZES
Small (Medium, Large). *Instructions are for smallest size, with changes for other sizes noted in parentheses as necessary.*

FINISHED MEASUREMENTS
Waist (before elastic is sewn in):
    27³/₄ (32, 36¹/₄)"
Length: 27"

MATERIALS
JCA/Reynolds Yarn's *Frisky* (4-worsted
    weight; 60% cotton/40% nylon; each
    approx 1³/₄ oz/50 g and 81 yd/74 m),
    14 (16, 18) balls of Purple Haze #13
One *each* of sizes 6 and 8 (4.00 and
    5.00 mm) circular knitting needles
    (24" long) or size needed to obtain
    gauge
Elastic, ³/₄" wide, cut to fit waist
Four stitch markers, one in a different
    color to be used to indicate beg of
    rounds
One blunt-end yarn needle

GAUGE
With larger circular needle in Stockinette St Patt Worked in the Round, 19 sts and 26 rnds = 4". *To save time, take time to check gauge.*

STITCH PATTERN
Stockinette Stitch Pattern Worked in the Round
(over any number of sts)
Patt Rnd: Knit around.

Repeat Patt Rnd for patt.

NOTES
Constructionwise, this skirt is made in the round from the bottom up.
When placing markers, use a different-colored marker to indicate the beginning of rounds.

Knit Notes
Be sure to cast on and bind off quite loosely when making this project or else the hems might pucker. Afraid you'll do so too tightly? Use knitting needles a size or two larger than your main knitting needles just for those cast-on and bind-off rows.

Cont even in Stockinette St Patt Worked in the Round until piece measures approx 26" from Lower Hem Turning Rnd.

Waistband Turning Rnd
Next Rnd: *K2tog, yarn over. Repeat from * around.

Change to smaller circular needle, and cont even in Stockinette St Patt Worked in the Round until piece measures approx 1" from Waistband Turning Rnd.

BO *loosely*.

FINISHING
Weave in any tails on WS, *except those to be used later in hemming*.

Fold lower edge of skirt to WS at Lower Hem Turning Rnd, and whipstitch *loosely* into place.

Cut elastic to the desired waist measurement plus approx 1". Overlap the ends of elastic and sew them together. Fold the waistband in half to WS at Waistband Turning Rnd, and insert the elastic.

Whipstitch waistband *loosely* into place on WS.

Weave in any remaining yarn tails to WS.

HEM FACING
With smaller circular needle, use cable cast on to CO 308 (328, 348) sts.

Join, *being careful not to twist sts*. Place stitch marker on needle to indicate beg of rnd and slip marker every rnd.

Beg Stockinette St Patt Worked in the Round, and cont even until piece measures approx 1" from beg.

Change to larger circular needle.

Lower Hem Turning Rnd
Next Rnd: *K2tog, yarn over. Repeat from * around.

Cont even in Stockinette St Patt Worked in the Round until piece measures approx 4" from Lower Hem Turning Rnd.

Next Rnd: *K29 (34, 39) sts, place marker, K48, place marker. Repeat from * around.

Next Rnd (Dec Rnd): *K29 (34, 39) sts, slip marker, SSK, knit across until 2 sts rem before next marker, K2tog, slip marker. Repeat from * around—300 (320, 340) sts rem—8 sts decreased.

Repeat Dec Rnd every sixth rnd twenty-one more times— 132 (152, 172) sts rem.

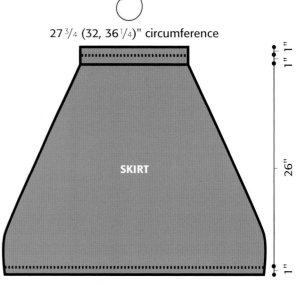

27 3/4 (32, 36 1/4)" circumference

SKIRT

1" 1"

26"

1"

65 (69, 73 1/4)" circumference

NOTE: THE DASHED LINES IN THIS ILLUSTRATION INDICATE THE POSITIONS OF HEMS.

shutting those eyelet holes

If you don't want a lacy look, you can eliminate those holes with a simple twist! This section shows you how to make them go away.

Knitting through the Back Loop

You learned the Yarn Over Increase in Lesson 9 on page 66, which is used to create decorative holes in knitted fabric (see the "Sarong" on page 70 for an example of this technique). If you don't want these holes, you can close them up as follows.

To close up the hole in a Yarn Over Increase, rather than insert the tip of the right-hand needle into the front loop of the stitch on the subsequent row as you knit it, position the right-hand needle *behind* the left-hand needle and insert the tip of it *into the back loop* of the stitch (see illustration below).

Twisting a Yarn Over Increase this way closes up the hole and makes this type of increase practically invisible!

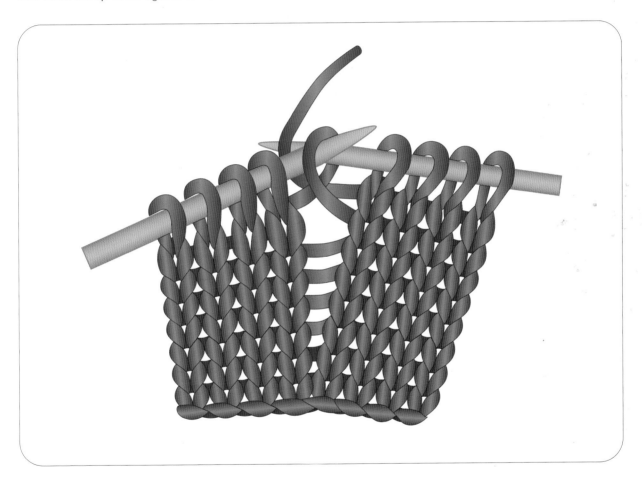

A-Line Pullover

This project requires practically no finishing once the knitting is complete. Made entirely in the round from the bottom up, its slightly flared silhouette is flattering and oh-so-comfy! And, while making the sleeves, you'll practice knitting through the back loop to close up the holes created by the yarn over increases.

SKILL LEVEL
2

BASIC STITCHES AND TECHNIQUES
Gauge
Cable Cast On
Knitting in the Round on a
    Circular Needle
Knitting in the Round on Double-Pointed
    Needles
Knit Stitch
Joining a New Yarn
Knit Two Together Decrease
Knit Three Together Decrease
Slip, Slip, Knit Decrease
Slip, Slip, Slip, Knit Decrease
Yarn Over Increase
Knitting through the Back Loop
Binding Off
Hiding Yarn Tails
Blocking
Whipstitch Seam

SIZES
Small (Medium, Large, 1X, 2X).
Instructions are for smallest size, with changes for other sizes noted in parentheses as necessary.

FINISHED MEASUREMENTS
Bust: 36 (38$\frac{1}{2}$, 42$\frac{1}{2}$, 45$\frac{1}{2}$, 49$\frac{1}{2}$)"
Length: 25 (25$\frac{1}{2}$, 26, 26$\frac{1}{2}$, 27)"

MATERIALS
Lorna's Laces's *Swirl Chunky* (5-bulky
    weight; 83% merino wool/17% silk;
    each approx 4 oz/113 g and 120 yd/
    110 m), 7 (8, 9, 10, 11) hanks
    of Poppy
One size 11 (8.00 mm) circular knitting
    needle (29" long) or size needed to
    obtain gauge
One size 11 (8.00 mm) circular knitting
    needle (16" long) or size needed to
    obtain gauge
One set of five size 11 (8.00 mm)
    double-pointed knitting needles or
    size needed to obtain gauge
Four stitch markers (one in a different
    color to be used to indicate beg
    of rnds)
Four stitch holders
One blunt-end yarn needle

GAUGE
In Stockinette St Patt Worked in the
Round, 12 sts and 16 rnds = 4".
*To save time, take time to check
gauge.*

STITCH PATTERN
Stockinette Stitch Pattern
Worked in the Round
(over any number of sts)
Patt Rnd: Knit around.

Repeat Patt Rnd for patt.

NOTES
Constructionwise, this sweater is
    worked in one piece from the
    bottom up.
When placing markers, use a different-
    colored marker to indicate the
    beginning of rounds.
**To prevent holes when increasing for
    the sleeves,** be sure to close up
    each yarn over increase by knitting
    through its back loop on the
    following round.
When knitting the raglan yoke, change
    to the shorter circular needle when
    there are too few stitches remaining
    to knit comfortably with the longer
    circular needle.
**Yoke Dec Rnd 1 (decreases 1 st at
    each side of sleeves, front, and
    back when making the raglan
    yoke):** *Slip marker, K1, SSK, knit
    across to 3 sts before next marker,
    K2tog, K1. Repeat from * three more
    times.
**Yoke Dec Rnd 2 (decreases 1 st at
    each side of sleeves and 2 sts at
    each side of front and back when
    making the raglan yoke):** *Slip
    marker, K1, SSK, knit across to 3 sts
    before next marker, K2tog, K1, slip
    marker, K1, SSSK, knit across until
    4 sts before next marker, K3tog, K1.
    Repeat from * once more.

BODY

With longer circular needle, use cable cast on to CO 140 (148, 160, 168, 180) sts.

Join, *being careful not to twist sts*. Place stitch marker on needle to indicate beg of rnd and slip marker every rnd.

Beg Stockinette St Patt Worked in the Round, and cont even until piece measures approx 4" from beg.

Next Rnd: K70 (74, 80, 84, 90) sts, place marker, knit around to end rnd.

Next Rnd (Decrease Rnd): *K2, SSK, knit around until 4 sts rem before next marker, K2tog, K2, slip marker. Repeat from * one more time—136 (144, 156, 164, 176) sts rem.

Work four rnds even.

Next Rnd: Repeat Dec Rnd—132 (140, 152, 160, 172) sts rem.

Knit Notes

This circularly knit sweater provides a great opportunity to use up your stash of yarn! Knit random stripes of various sizes, beginning and ending each stripe at your whim. Don't worry about matching the stripes on both sleeves. The variation will add to the color play and make your sweater a true original!

Repeat Dec Rnd every fifth rnd six *more* times— 108 (116, 128, 136, 148) sts rem.

Cont even in patt as established until piece measures approx 16 1/2" from beg, ending last rnd 3 sts rem before marker.

Armhole Shaping

BO 6 sts, work across to 3 sts rem before marker, BO 6 sts, work across to end. Slip sts onto stitch holder.

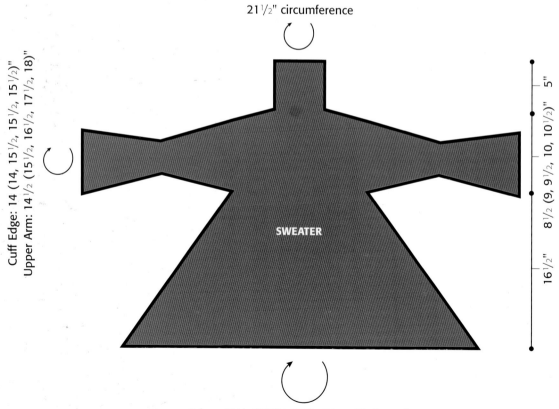

21 1/2" circumference

Cuff Edge: 14 (14, 15 1/2, 15 1/2, 15 1/2)"
Upper Arm: 14 1/2 (15 1/2, 16 1/2, 17 1/2, 18)"

5"

8 1/2 (9, 9 1/2, 10, 10 1/2)"

16 1/2"

SWEATER

Lower Edge: 46 1/2 (48 1/2, 53 1/2, 56, 60)" circumference
Bust: 36 (38 1/2, 42 1/2, 45 1/2, 49 1/2)" circumference

SLEEVE
(Make two)

With shorter circular needle, use cable cast on to CO 42 (42, 46, 46, 46) sts.

Divide sts evenly and slide onto four dpns.

Join, *being careful not to twist sts*. Place marker on needle to indicate beg of rnd and slip marker every rnd.

Beg Stockinette St Patt Worked in the Round, and cont even until piece measures approx 3" from beg.

Next Rnd (Dec Rnd): K2, SSK, knit around until 4 sts rem before next marker, K2tog, K2, slip marker.

Repeat Dec Rnd every eighth rnd three *more* times— 34 (34, 38, 38, 38) sts rem.

Cont even in patt as established until piece measures approx 10 1/2" from beg.

Next Rnd (Inc Rnd): K2, yarn over, knit around until 2 sts rem before marker, yarn over, K2.

Remembering to knit all yarn overs *through the loop* on successive rnds (see Notes), rep Inc Rnd every other rnd 0 (0, 0, 1, 3) times, every fourth row 2 (5, 5, 5, 4) times, then every sixth row 2 (0, 0, 0, 0) times—44 (46, 50, 52, 54) sts.

Cont even in patt as established until piece measures approx 17 1/2" from beg, ending last rnd 3 sts before marker.

Next Rnd: BO 3 sts, work across to 3 sts rem before marker, BO 3 sts, work across to end. Slip 38 (40, 44, 46, 48) sts onto holder.

RAGLAN YOKE
Next Rnd (Joining Rnd): K38 (40, 44, 46, 48) sts from one sleeve holder, place marker, K48 (52, 58, 62, 68) sts from front holder, place marker, K38 (40, 44, 46, 48) sts from second sleeve holder, place marker, K48 (52, 58, 62, 68) sts from back holder, place different-colored marker—172 (184, 204, 216, 232) sts.

Work 1 (0, 2, 1, 0) rnds even.

Cont patt as established, *and at the same time,* work Yoke Dec Rnd 1 (see Notes) every third rnd 6 (6, 1, 1, 0) times, then work Yoke Dec Rnd 2 (see Notes) every third rnd 5 (6, 1, 1, 0) times—64 sts rem.

Cont even in patt for 5".

BO *loosely*.

FINISHING
Weave in any tails on WS, *except those to be used later in seaming.*

Block pieces to measurements.

Whipstitch underarm seams.

Weave in any remaining yarn tails to WS.

pick up sticks—
i mean
stitches

Often, to add a neckband or border, you must create new stitches along the edge of the fabric, then knit them. You'll learn how here.

Picking Up Stitches

During the course of a project you might be instructed to pick up stitches along horizontal and/or vertical edges. Picking up live, knittable stitches on an already-knit fabric can be a trial-and-error process, even for veteran knitters, so take your time as you work. And remember, you can always rip back if you're not happy with the results!

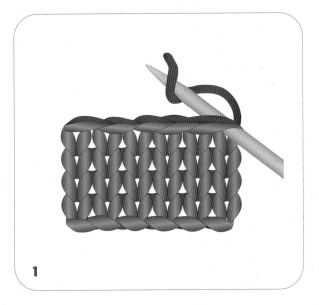

1

Knit Notes

When picking up stitches, it's best to position the knitted piece so that the right side is facing you. This way, you can eliminate any unsightly bunching or holes as you go. And if you're picking up lots of stitches, use a circular knitting needle (see "Needles" on page 12) so that you can accommodate all those stitches on the needle.

PICKING UP STITCHES ALONG A HORIZONTAL EDGE

1 To pick up stitches along the *bound-off edge* of a piece of knitted fabric, insert a knitting needle *into the middle* of the first stitch just below the bind-off. Be sure to go into the center of the "V," not into the links of the chain running along the top of the fabric.

2 Wrap the yarn around the needle *knitwise* (see illustration 1).

3 Use the tip of the needle to pull up a loop, creating a stitch.

4 Continue in this manner, picking up one stitch in each stitch (see illustration 2).

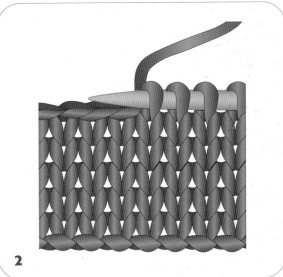

2

PICKING UP STITCHES ALONG A VERTICAL EDGE

1 To pick up stitches along the *side* of a piece of knitted fabric, insert a knitting needle *between the first and second stitches* in the first row of knitting. Do not insert the needle in the middle of a "V" but rather between two stitches. To find the space between the two stitches, just look for the horizontal strand that's running between stitches.

2 Wrap the yarn around the needle *knitwise* (see illustration 1).

3 Use the tip of the needle to pull up a loop, creating a stitch.

4 Continue in this manner along the edge (see illustration 2).

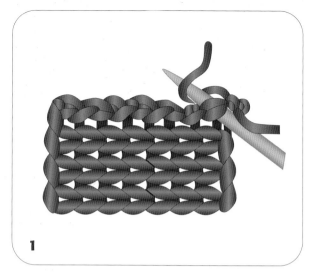

1

Knit Notes

Here are some pick-up-stitch tips.

- When picking up stitches on a vertical edge of stockinette stitch fabric, pick up one stitch in each of three rows *and then skip one row (or horizontal strand)* (see illustration 2). If you pick up a stitch in every row of stockinette stitch fabric rather than in three out of every four rows along the edge, you'll get a rippled border because of the difference in dimensions between the stitch gauge and the row gauge. In garter stitch fabric, because of the relationship between its stitch and row gauge, you can pick up one stitch for every two rows (or one ridge).

- When working along a curved edge, be careful where you insert the knitting needle to pick up stitches. Try to do so just inside the shaped edge. *If you notice a slight hole in the knitted fabric, avoid picking up a stitch in that particular area* since doing so will actually accentuate the hole rather than hide it!

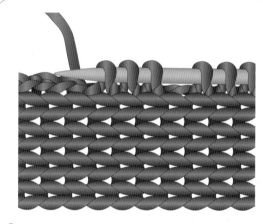

2

Stripes-on-the-Move Pullover

With its vertical lines, this sweater is particularly flattering. The front and back pieces consist of a single mitered square, and horizontal stripes are added to create the yoke. For quick and easy finishing, its sleeves are picked up and knitted downward.

SKILL LEVEL
2

BASIC STITCHES AND TECHNIQUES
Gauge
Cable Cast On
Knit Stitch
Joining a New Yarn
Alternating between Two Balls of Yarn
Knit Two Together Decrease
Slip, Slip, Knit Decrease
Picking Up Stitches
Binding Off
Hiding Yarn Tails
Blocking
Horizontal-to-Horizontal Invisible Weave
    Seam
Vertical-to-Vertical Invisible Weave Seam

SIZES
Small (Medium, Large, 1X, 2X).
Instructions are for smallest size, with changes for other sizes noted in parentheses as necessary.

FINISHED MEASUREMENTS
Bust: 37 (41, 44^1/$_2$, 48, 51^1/$_2$)"
Length: 22 (24, 25, 25^3/$_4$, 26^3/$_4$)"

MATERIALS
South West Trading Company's *Phoenix*
    (4-worsted weight; 100% Soy Silk™;
    each approx 3^1/$_2$ oz/100 g and
    175 yd/160 m), 6 (6, 7, 7, 8) balls
    of Pretty in Pink #506-PNK (A)
South West Trading Company's *Fur Real*
    (5-bulky weight; 58% nylon/30%
    rayon/12% acrylic; each approx 1^3/$_4$
    oz/50 g and 80 yd/73 m), 5 (6, 6, 7,
    7) balls of Pink Elephant #555-7 (B)
South West Trading Company's *Calypso*
    (4-worsted weight; 70% rayon/
    20% acrylic/10% polyester; each
    approx 1^3/$_4$ oz/50 g and 109 yd/
    100 m), 5 (6, 6, 7, 7) balls of
    Bougainvillea #550-7 (C)
One pair of size 8 (5.00 mm) knitting
    needles or size needed to obtain
    gauge
One stitch marker
One blunt-end yarn needle

GAUGE
In Garter St Patt in Stripe Sequence,
18 sts and 36 rows = 4". *To save time, take time to check gauge.*

STITCH PATTERN
Garter Stitch Pattern
(over any number of sts)
Patt Row: Knit across.

Repeat Patt Row.
Stripe Sequence
Four rows *each* of *A, B, A, C. Repeat from * for patt.

NOTES
Constructionwise, the lower portion of the front and back of this sweater are made from a mitered square in which two sides of the square are cast on and then decreases are worked in the center until no more stitches remain. The yoke is created by picking up stitches along one side of the square and knitting upward. The sleeves are picked up around the armhole and worked downward.

For ease in finishing, do not cut yarn at end of stripes; rather, carry it *loosely* up side of work on WS.

For sweater assembly, refer to the illustration for drop-shoulder construction on page 126.

Knit Notes
When picking up stitches along a cast-on (or bind-off) edge, always work *into the top stitch* and not into the edge loop forming the cast-on (or bind-off).

BACK

With A, use cable cast on to CO 168 (184, 200, 216, 232) sts. Place a stitch marker after the 84th (92nd, 100th, 108th, 116th) st.

Row 1 (RS): With A, knit across until 2 sts rem before marker, SSK, slip marker, K2tog, knit across to end row.

Row 2 and all WS rows: With same color as previous row, knit across.

Repeat Rows 1 and 2 in Stripe Sequence until 2 sts rem, ending after RS row.

Next Row (WS): SSK.

Fasten off.

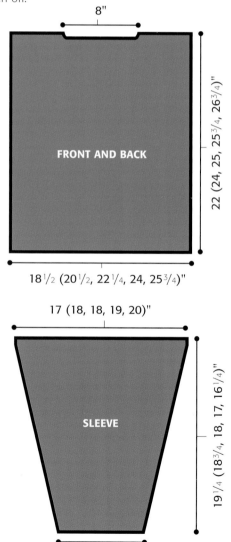

8"

FRONT AND BACK

22 (24, 25, 25³/₄, 26³/₄)"

18¹/₂ (20¹/₂, 22¹/₄, 24, 25³/₄)"

17 (18, 18, 19, 20)"

SLEEVE

19¹/₄ (18³/₄, 18, 17, 16¹/₄)"

9"

YOKE

Turn mitered square so cast-on edge runs along the top and right-hand sides (see photograph at right). With RS facing and C, pick up and knit 84 (92, 100, 108, 116) sts along upper edge.

Cont even in Garter St Patt and Stripe Sequence until piece measures approx 21 1/2 (23 1/2, 24 1/2, 25 1/4, 26 1/4)" from beg, ending after WS row.

Shape Neck

Next Row (RS): Cont Stripe Sequence as established, K28 (32, 36, 40, 44) sts; join second ball of yarn and BO middle 28 sts, knit across to end row.

Next Row: K26 (30, 34, 38, 42) sts, K2tog; on second side of neck, with second ball of yarn, SSK, knit across to end row.

Next Row: K25 (29, 33, 37, 41) sts, K2tog; on second side of neck, with second ball of yarn, SSK, knit across to end row.

Next Row: K24 (28, 32, 36, 40) sts, K2tog; on second side of neck, with second ball of yarn, SSK, knit across to end row.

Next Row: K23 (27, 31, 35, 39) sts, K2tog; on second side of neck, with second ball of yarn, SSK, knit across to end row.

Cont even in patt as established, if necessary, until piece measures approx 22 (24, 25, 25 3/4, 26 3/4)" from beg, ending after RS row.

Next Row (WS): Knit and BO.

FRONT

Same as back.

SLEEVES

Use horizontal-to-horizontal invisible weave seams to sew shoulder seams.

Place markers 8 1/2 (9, 9, 9 1/2, 10)" down from shoulders.

With RS facing and C, pick up and knit 78 (82, 82, 86, 92) sts between markers.

Beg Garter St Patt and Stripe Sequence, **and at the same time**, dec 1 st each side every tenth row 9 (0, 0, 0, 0) times, every eighth row 9 (18, 15, 4, 0) times, every sixth row 0 (2, 5, 18, 17) times, then every fourth row 0 (0, 0, 0, 8) times—42 sts rem.

Cont even in patt as established until sleeve measures approx 19 1/4 (18 3/4, 18, 17, 16 1/4)" from beg.

BO.

Repeat for second sleeve.

FINISHING

Weave in any tails on WS, *except those to be used later in seaming*.

Block pieces to measurements.

Use vertical-to-vertical invisible weave seams to sew sleeve and side seams.

Weave in any remaining yarn tails to WS.

Big, Easy Jacket

Now here's a jacket that you can live in! Wear it to the office, to the soccer game, or just to cozy up to a fire on a winter's day. It's quick to knit, with sleeves knit at the same time as the body. The dramatic fold-over lapel is picked up and knitted at the very end.

SKILL LEVEL
2

BASIC STITCHES AND TECHNIQUES
Gauge
Cable Cast On
Knit Stitch
Joining a New Yarn
Alternating between Two Balls of Yarn
Knit Two Together Decrease
Yarn Over Increase
Knitting through the Back Loop
Picking Up Stitches
Binding Off
Hiding Yarn Tails
Blocking
Horizontal-to-Horizontal Invisible Weave
    Seam
Vertical-to-Vertical Invisible Weave Seam
Vertical-to-Horizontal Invisible Weave
    Seam

SIZES
Small/Medium (Large/1X). *Instructions are for smaller size, with changes for other sizes noted in parentheses as necessary.*

FINISHED MEASUREMENTS
Bust: 46 (54)"
Length: 33 (34)"

MATERIALS
JCA/Artful Yarn's *Circus* (6-super bulky weight; 95% wool/5% acrylic; each approx 3 1/2 oz/100 g and 93 yd/85 m), 15 (18) balls of Family of Acrobats #05

One pair of size 11 (8.00 mm) knitting needles or size needed to obtain gauge
One size 11 (8.00 mm) circular knitting needle (36" long) or size needed to obtain gauge
One stitch marker
One blunt-end yarn needle

GAUGE
In Garter St Patt, 10 sts and 20 rows = 4".
To save time, take time to check gauge.

STITCH PATTERN
Garter Stitch Pattern
(over any number of sts)
Patt Row: Knit across.

Repeat Patt Row.

NOTE
Constructionwise, this jacket is made in three pieces (two fronts and a back), with its dolman-like sleeves incorporated into the body.

Knit Notes
If you'd prefer a longer, duster length for your jacket, work more rows before beginning the increases for the sleeves. So simple!

BACK

Use cable cast on to CO 57 (67) sts.

Beg Garter St Patt, and work even until piece measures approx 20½ (21½)" from beg.

Increase for Sleeves

Next Row: Use cable cast on to CO 3 (4) sts at beg of next two rows—63 (75) sts.

Next Row: Use cable cast on to CO 5 (6) sts at beg of next two rows—73 (87) sts.

Next Row: Use cable cast on to CO 10 (7) sts at beg of next two rows—93 (101) sts.

Next Row: Use cable cast on to CO 15 (13) sts at beg of next two rows—123 (127) sts.

Next Row: Use cable cast on to CO 20 sts at beg of next two rows—163 (167) sts.

Cont even until piece measures approx 33 (34)" from beg.

BO *loosely*.

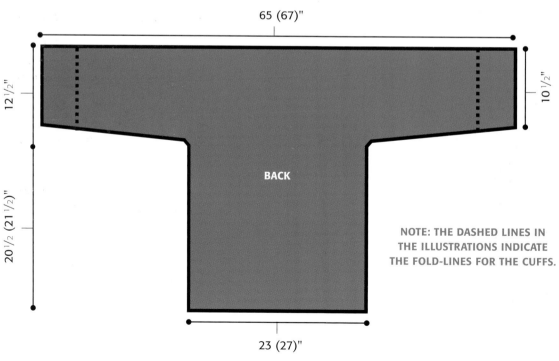

65 (67)"

12½"

10½"

BACK

20½ (21½)"

23 (27)"

NOTE: THE DASHED LINES IN THE ILLUSTRATIONS INDICATE THE FOLD-LINES FOR THE CUFFS.

LEFT FRONT

Use cable cast on to CO 21 (26) sts.

Beg Garter St Patt, and work even until piece measures approx 20 1/2 (21 1/2)" from beg.

Increase for Sleeves

Next Row: Use cable cast on to CO 3 (4) sts at beg of next row—24 (30) sts.

Next Row: Work one row even.

Next Row: Use cable cast on to CO 5 (6) sts at beg of next row—29 (36) sts.

Next Row: Work one row even.

Next Row: Use cable cast on to CO 10 (7) sts at beg of row—39 (43) sts.

Next Row: Work one row even.

Next Row: Use cable cast on to CO 15 (13) sts at beg of next row—54 (56) sts.

Next Row: Work one row even.

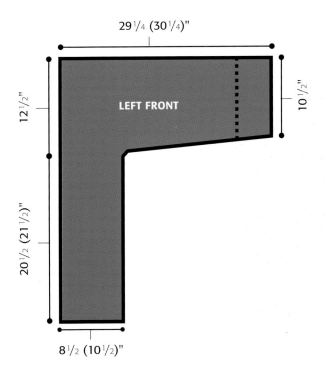

29 1/4 (30 1/4)"

12 1/2"

10 1/2"

LEFT FRONT

20 1/2 (21 1/2)"

8 1/2 (10 1/2)"

Next Row: Use cable cast on to CO 20 sts at beg of next row—74 (76) sts.

Cont even until piece measures approx 33 (34)" from beg.

BO *loosely*.

RIGHT FRONT

Same as left front.

FINISHING

Weave in any tails on WS, *except those to be used later in seaming.*

Block pieces to measurements.

Use horizontal-to-horizontal invisible weave seams to sew shoulder seams.

Collar and Front Bands

With RS facing and circular needle, beg at lower right front edge and pick up and knit 83 (85) sts evenly along right front edge, 15 sts along back of neck, and 83 (85) sts along left front edge—181 (185) sts total.

Place stitch marker in the fabric at center back of neck.

Work Garter St Patt, working a yarn over increase at center back of neck where marked every sixth row three times, being sure to knit the increased sts *through the back loop* on subsequent rows to prevent holes—184 (188) sts.

Cont even until band measures approx 6" from beg.

BO.

Use a combination of vertical-to-vertical and vertical-to-horizontal invisible weave seams to sew side and sleeve seams.

Fold up 4" of sleeve for cuff.

Weave in any remaining yarn tails to WS.

the second basic stitch of knitting

By now you've mastered the most basic stitch of knitting—the knit stitch—and learned lots of techniques (and made several projects!) using it. So let's turn to the purl stitch—the *second* basic stitch of knitting.

Making the Purl Stitch

The purl stitch is the reverse of the knit stitch, so that the right side of one stitch is identical to the wrong side of the other. All knitted fabrics are made from just these two stitches and their variations. Once you've learned the knit stitch *and* the purl stitch, there's nothing you can't do! Even increasing and decreasing while purling will be easy for you since you've practiced these maneuvers with the knit stitch. Let's give purling a go!

1 To make a purl stitch, place the needle with the cast-on stitches in your left hand. Hold the empty needle in your right hand.

Keeping the working yarn in front as you work, insert the tip of the right-hand knitting needle into the first stitch on the left-hand needle *from back to front and from right to left*.

Wrap the working yarn from right to left, and over and under, the tip of the right-hand needle (see illustration 1).

2 Use the right-hand needle to catch the yarn and pull it through the first stitch on the left-hand needle (see illustration 2).

3 Drop the first stitch off the left-hand needle and leave the new purl stitch on the right-hand needle (see illustration 3).

To complete the row of purl stitches, repeat these steps until the left-hand needle is empty.

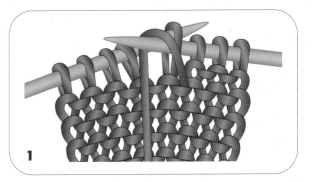

1

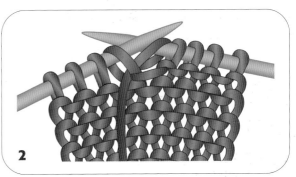

2

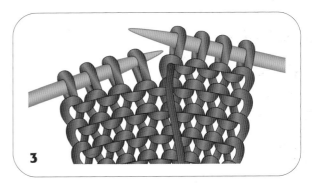

3

Knit Notes

"Purlwise" and "knitwise"— what's the difference? When purling, the right-hand knitting needle is inserted into stitches purlwise *(from right to left)* (see illustration 1) instead of knitwise *(from left to right)* (see illustration 2).

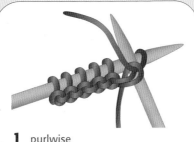

1 purlwise

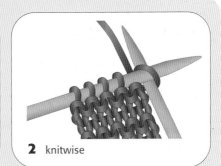

2 knitwise

PURL STITCH VARIATIONS

The purl stitch is a valuable skill to add to your knitter's backpack since the combination of knit and purl stitches can create an endless variety of textured fabrics. Here are some common ones.

Stockinette Stitch

Stockinette stitch is one of the most common knitted fabrics. As you can see in the photo at right, it's smooth on the right side (where all the knit stitches are) and bumpy on the wrong side (where the purl stitches are). You've already made stockinette stitch fabric by knitting all the stitches while working in the round. To create the same stockinette stitch fabric while working back and forth in rows, simply alternate one row of knit stitches with one row of purl stitches!

Reverse Stockinette Stitch

Reverse stockinette stitch is simply the back side of stockinette stitch. It appears bumpy on the right side (due to the purl stitches) and looks smooth on the wrong side (due to the knit stitches). (See the right-hand tie in the same photo for an example of what this stitch looks like.) It's worked the same way as stockinette stitch, alternating one row of knit stitches with one row of purl stitches—but the purl side of the fabric is the right side.

Ribbing

In ribbed fabrics, knit and purl stitches are alternated across a row, with knit stitches stacked on top of knit stitches and purl stitches stacked on top of purls (see photograph at bottom right). It's this vertical alignment of stitches that creates the elastic quality of ribbed fabrics, making them great for places where you want stretch in a garment (the cuffs and neckband, for instance). Many ribbed stitch patterns are possible, but Knit One Purl One Rib and Knit Two Purl Two Rib are the most common. The "Ribbed Cami" on page 115 is yet another ribbed variation.

Knit Notes

When knitting a ribbed fabric, be careful to bring the working yarn *between the needles*—not over the right-hand needle—when switching from knit to purl and from purl to knit. Otherwise you might inadvertently make a yarn over on the right-hand needle and create a hole in your fabric!

Purl Stitch Decreases, Part One

Just as there are different types of decreases with the knit stitch, there are several types for the purl stitch as well. Here are some of them to get you started. (You'll learn more in Lesson 15 on page 112.)

RIGHT-SLANTING PURL STITCH DECREASES

Knitters like to do all their exciting maneuvers—such as shaping—on right-side rows whenever possible. However, occasionally one must decrease on wrong-side rows. In these cases, it's handy to be able to make purl decreases that slant in a particular direction (in order to match Knit Two Together and Slip, Slip, Knit Decreases).

Here's how to make purl decreases that slant to the right on the public side of the fabric.

Purl Two Together Decrease

This decrease is the easiest one to make while purling. To do it, you'll combine two purl stitches into one as follows.

With the working yarn in front, insert the tip of the right-hand needle into the first two stitches on the left-hand needle *purlwise, from right to left*, as if they were a single stitch. Wrap the yarn around the right-hand needle as you would for a purl stitch, pull the yarn through both stitches, and purl a stitch, slipping both stitches off the left-hand needle at once (see illustration below).

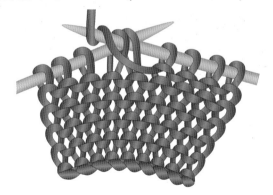

See? One stitch has been decreased, *and the resulting stitch slants to the right on the knit side of the fabric.*

Purl Three Together Decrease

To decrease two stitches at once, insert the right-hand needle into three stitches instead of two, as follows.

With the working yarn in front, insert the tip of the right-hand needle into the first three stitches on the left-hand needle *purlwise, from right to left*, as if they were a single stitch. Wrap the yarn around the right-hand needle as you would for a purl stitch, pull the yarn through all three stitches, and purl a stitch, slipping the three stitches off the left-hand needle at once (see illustration at right).

Here, two stitches have been decreased, *and the resulting stitch slants to the right on the knit side of the fabric.*

LEFT-SLANTING PURL STITCH DECREASES

Sometimes you'll want to make purl decreases that slant to the left on the knit side of the fabric. Here's how.

Purl Two Together through Back Loop Decrease

To make this left-slanting purl decrease, insert the right-hand needle into stitches from a new position—*from back to front and through the second stitch first and then through the first one*. Sure, it sounds awkward just reading it, but it isn't hard once you try it!

Insert the tip of the right-hand needle into the first two stitches on the left-hand needle *from back to front and from left to right*. Be sure to insert the tip of the needle into the second stitch on the left-hand needle first and then into the first stitch (see illustration above right).

You've combined two purl stitches into one, and the resulting stitch slants to the left on the knit side of the fabric. It's useful when you want to mimic the look of a Slip, Slip, Knit Decrease while working on the wrong side.

Oops! Fixing Common Mistakes, Part Two

An important part of mastering a new skill is learning how to fix errors. If you notice a problem with your fabric, don't panic! You'll probably be able to correct the mistake without having to rip everything out. You'll learn how to troubleshoot common errors in this section.

CORRECTING DROPPED STITCHES IN STOCKINETTE STITCH

Occasionally a stitch may drop off your knitting needle without you noticing it immediately. When this happens, you can add it back onto your needle without too much trouble.

Dropped Knit Stitch

1 If a single knit stitch has dropped down one row, position the knitting so that its right side is facing you, with the dropped stitch *in front of* the loose horizontal strand of yarn (see illustration 1).

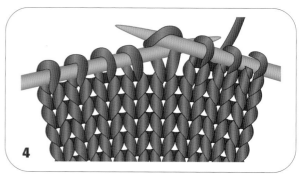

2 Then, insert the right-hand knitting needle first through the dropped stitch and then under the loose yarn (see illustration 2).

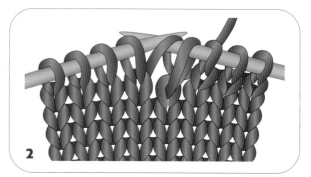

3 Use the left-hand needle to lift the dropped stitch *over* the loose strand of yarn and off the right-hand needle (see illustration 3).

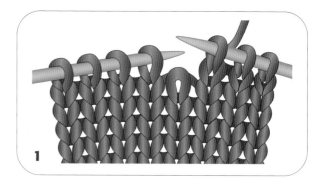

4 Finally, slip the new stitch that's on the right-hand needle back onto the left-hand needle. As you transfer the stitch, insert the left-hand needle into it *from front to back and from left to right* (see illustration 4).

If more than one stitch has been dropped, fix them one at a time.

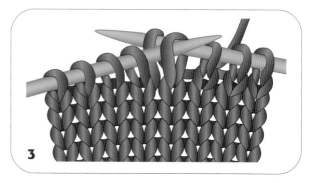

Dropped Purl Stitch

1 If a single purl stitch has dropped down one row, position the knitting so that the purl side is facing you, with the dropped stitch toward the back of the fabric and the loose yarn toward the front (see illustration 1).

2 Then, insert the right-hand knitting needle *from back to front*, first through the dropped stitch and then under the loose yarn (see illustration 2).

3 Use the left-hand needle to lift the dropped stitch *over* the loose strand of yarn and off the right-hand needle (see illustration 3).

4 Finally, slip the new stitch that's on the right-hand needle back onto the left-hand needle. As you transfer the stitch, insert the left-hand needle into it *from front to back and from left to right* (see illustration 4).

If more than one stitch has been dropped, fix them one at a time.

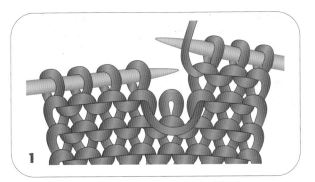

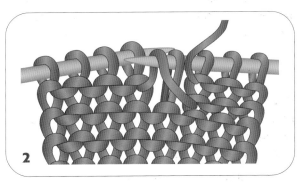

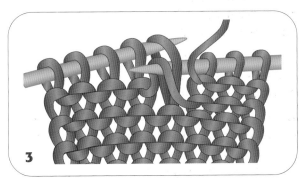

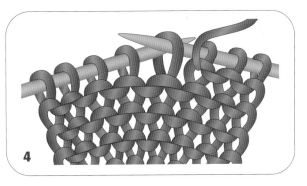

RESCUING RUNNING STITCHES

If a stitch has raveled down several rows of stockinette stitch, you can easily use a crochet hook to link it back up!

With the knit side of the fabric toward you *and the loose stitch in front of the fabric*, insert a crochet hook into the dropped stitch *from front to back*, catch the first horizontal strand, and draw it through (see illustration 1). Repeat until all the strands have been hooked.

UNRAVELING PURL STITCHES TO RIP OUT A PARTIAL ROW

Sometimes you'll need to rip out a row of your knitting one stitch at a time while you are on a purl row. Relax. It's really not that difficult!

To unravel a purl stitch, keep the yarn in front of the fabric, then insert the left-hand needle *from front to back and from left to right* into the first stitch on the right-hand needle—the one just below the live stitch that's sitting on the needle (see illustration 2).

Let the stitch drop and unravel the stitch by gently tugging on the working yarn.

UNRAVELING PURL STITCHES TO RIP OUT AN ENTIRE ROW

If you must rip out an entire row (or more) of stitches, simply remove the knitting needle and pull on the working yarn. If you're removing multiple rows, stop with the row above the offending row, then rip out the last row *stitch by stitch*. The important part is placing the live stitches back on the needle correctly as follows.

When replacing purl stitches back on the knitting needle, insert the tip of the needle into each stitch *from back to front*, making sure that the right "leg" of each stitch is to the front of the needle (see illustration 3).

That wasn't hard, was it?

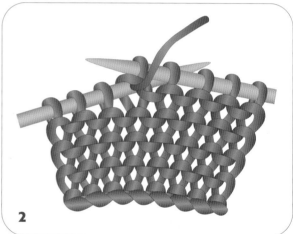

1

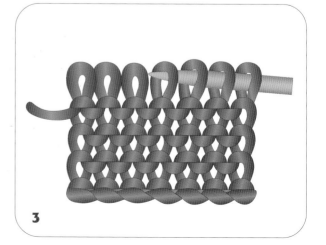

2

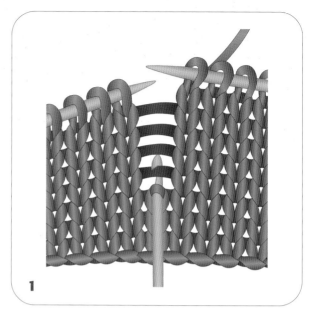

3

Plush Pullover

You'll have this sporty top knitted up in no time, thanks to the bulky weight yarn. All its texture will hide any tiny imperfections as you practice the purl stitch!

SKILL LEVEL
2

BASIC STITCHES AND TECHNIQUES
Gauge
Cable Cast On
Knit Stitch
Purl Stitch
Joining a New Yarn
Knit Two Together Decrease
Slip, Slip, Knit Decrease
Purl Two Together Decrease
Purl Two Together through the Back
  Loops Decrease
Binding Off
Hiding Yarn Tails
Blocking
Whipstitch Seam
Picking Up Stitches

SIZES
Small (Medium, Large, 1X, 2X, 3X).
Instructions are for smallest size, with changes for other sizes noted in parentheses as necessary.

FINISHED MEASUREMENTS
Bust: 36 (40, 44, 48, 52, 56)"
Length: 18 (18 1/2, 18 3/4, 19 1/4, 19 1/2, 19 1/2)"

MATERIALS
Knit One Crochet Too's *Fleece* (5-bulky
  weight; 100% polyester; each
  approx 1 3/4 oz/50 g and 109 yd/
  100 m), 3 (4, 4, 5, 5, 6) balls of
  Coral #353
One pair *each* of sizes 7 and 9 (4.50
  and 5.50 mm) knitting needles or
  size needed to obtain gauge
One blunt-end yarn needle

GAUGE
With larger needles in Stockinette St Patt,
12 sts and 20 rows = 4". *To save time, take time to check gauge.*

STITCH PATTERNS
Garter Stitch Pattern
(over any number of sts)
Patt Row: Knit across.

Repeat Patt Row.
Stockinette Stitch Pattern
(over any number of sts)
Row 1 (RS): Knit across.

Row 2: Purl across.

Repeat Rows 1 and 2 for patt.

NOTES
For ease in finishing, instructions
  include one selvage stitch each side;
  these stitches are not reflected in
  final measurements.
For fully-fashioned armhole decreases:
  on RS rows, K1, SSK, work across in
  patt as established until 3 sts rem in
  row, ending row with K2tog, K1; *on
  WS rows,* P1, P2tog, work across in
  patt as established until 3 sts rem in
  row, ending row with P2tog through
  back loops, P1.
**For fully-fashioned neckline decreases
  on left side of neck:** *on RS rows,*
  work across until 3 sts rem in row,
  ending row with K2tog, K1; *on WS
  rows,* P1, P2tog, then purl across to
  end row.
**For fully-fashioned neckline decreases
  on right side of neck:** *on RS rows,*
  K1, SSK, then knit across to end row;
  on WS rows, purl across until 3 sts
  rem in row, ending row with P2tog
  through back loops, P1.

BACK

With smaller needles, use cable cast on to CO 56 (62, 68, 74, 80, 86) sts.

Beg Garter St Patt, and work even until piece measures approx 1½" from beg, ending after WS row.

Change to larger needles, and beg Stockinette St Patt.

Cont even until piece measures approx 10 (10, 10, 10½, 10½, 10½)" from beg, ending after WS row.

Shape Armholes

BO 4 (5, 6, 7, 9, 10) sts at beg of next two rows—48 (52, 56, 60, 62, 66) sts rem.

Work fully-fashioned decreases (see Notes) each side every row 3 (6, 6, 9, 9, 12) times, then every other row 2 (1, 2, 1, 1, 0) times—38 (38, 40, 40, 42, 42) sts rem.

Cont even until piece measures approx 17 (17½, 17¾, 18¼, 18½, 18½)" from beg, ending after WS row.

Shape Shoulders

BO 3 (3, 3, 3, 4, 4) sts at beg of next four rows, then BO 3 (3, 4, 4, 3, 3) sts at beg of next two rows—20 sts rem.

BO.

FRONT

Same as back until piece measures approx 11½ (12, 12¼, 12¾, 13, 13)" from beg, ending after WS row.

Divide for Neck Slit

Work across first 18 (18, 19, 19, 20, 20) sts; slip middle 2 sts onto safety pin; join second ball of yarn and work across to end row.

Work both sides at once with separate balls of yarn until piece measures approx 15½ (16, 16¼, 16¾, 17, 17)" from beg, ending after WS row.

Knit Notes

You can totally change the look of this pullover by substituting yarns. Choose super-soft angora or a metallic/mohair mélange for glitz and glam!

Shape Neck

BO 4 sts each neck edge once, then BO 2 sts each neck edge once—12 (12, 13, 13, 14, 14) sts rem each side.

Dec 1 st each neck edge every row three times, working fully-fashioned decreases on both the left and right side of the neck (see Notes)—9 (9, 10, 10, 11, 11) sts rem each side.

Cont even, if necessary, until piece measures same as back to shoulders.

Shape Shoulders

BO 3 (3, 3, 3, 4, 4) sts each shoulder edge two times, then BO rem 3 (3, 4, 4, 3, 3) sts.

FINISHING

Weave in any tails on WS, *except those to be used later in seaming.*

Block pieces to measurements.

Use whipstitch to sew shoulder seams.

Collar

With RS facing and smaller needles, pick up and knit 52 sts around neckline.

Beg Garter St Patt, and cont even until collar measures approx 4" from beg.

BO.

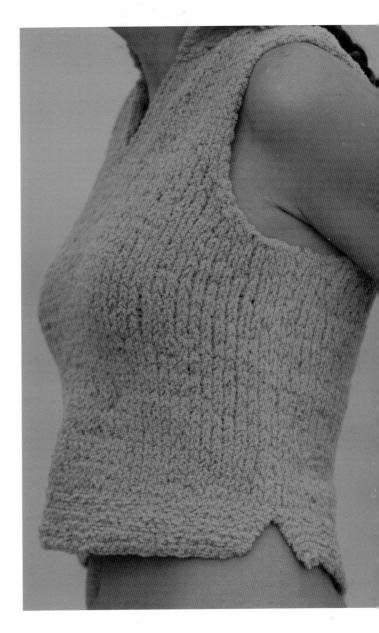

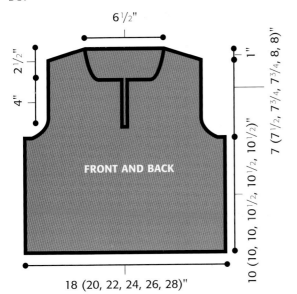

6½"

2½"

4"

1"

7 (7½, 7¾, 7¾, 8, 8)"

10 (10, 10½, 10½, 10½)"

FRONT AND BACK

18 (20, 22, 24, 26, 28)"

Neck Slit Edging

With RS facing and smaller needles, beg at left neck edge, and pick up and knit 11 sts along each side of neck slit plus 2 sts from safety pin—24 sts total.

Next Row (WS): Knit and BO.

Use whipstitch to sew side seams, leaving 1½" open at lower edge for side slits.

Weave in any remaining yarn tails to WS.

invisible (but oh-so-easy) seams, part two

In Lesson 6 on page 46 I mentioned the importance of choosing the best seaming method for every task. For stockinette stitch projects— and for most fabrics other than garter stitch—mattress stitch seams are the ones you'll want to use.

Gorgeous (I Mean Invisible) Seams on Stockinette Stitch Fabric

Mattress stitch seams are smooth, neat, and invisible! Use the mattress stitch seam (or invisible weave) technique for invisible seams in projects knitted in stockinette stitch fabric. This lesson shows you how to sew mattress stitch seams in different situations.

VERTICAL-TO-VERTICAL MATTRESS STITCH SEAMS

This type of seam is useful for side seams of garments knitted in stockinette stitch.

1 To make this type of seam, lay the pieces of fabric flat, side by side, and with right side of the fabric facing you—matching stripes, if applicable.

2 Thread a blunt-end yarn needle with the seaming yarn, leaving a 6" tail, and bring the needle up *from front to back to front* through the left-hand piece of fabric, going one stitch in from the side edge.

3 Bring the needle up *from front to back to front* through the corresponding spot on the right-hand piece, securing the lower edges together.

4 Insert the needle down, *from front to back, into the same place on the left-hand piece where the needle emerged before*, and bring it up through the corresponding place in the next row of fabric, grabbing the horizontal bar that is between the stitches.

5 Insert the needle down *from front to back into the same place on the right-hand piece where the needle emerged before*, and bring it up through the corresponding place in the next row of fabric, grabbing the horizontal bar between the stitches.

6 Repeat these steps, grabbing the horizontal bars between the stitches, until you've sewn a couple of inches. Then pull firmly on the sewing yarn, bringing the two pieces of knitting together. The edge stitch of each piece of stockinette stitch fabric will roll to the wrong side.

7 Continue this way until the seam is complete (see illustration below). Cut the yarn, leaving a 6" tail to be woven in later.

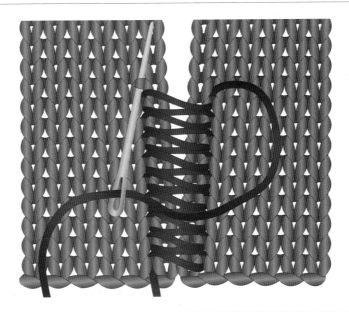

HORIZONTAL-TO-HORIZONTAL MATTRESS STITCH SEAMS

This type of seam is useful for shoulder seams of garments knitted in stockinette stitch.

1 To make this type of seam, lay the two pieces of fabric flat with the right side of the fabric facing you, with the bound-off edges together, placing one piece above the other.

2 Thread a blunt-end yarn needle with the seaming yarn, leave a 6″ tail, and bring the needle up *from back to front* through the center of the first stitch on the right-hand edge of the piece of fabric at the bottom just below the bound-off edge.

3 Insert the needle *from front to back to front and from right to left* into the center of the first stitch on the piece of fabric at the top just above the bound-off edge.

4 Bring the needle down *from front to back* into the center of the first stitch on the bottom piece of fabric just below the bound-off edge. Then bring it up through the center of the next stitch to the left.

5 Go back to the piece of fabric at the top, insert the needle down *into the same place it emerged before*, and bring it up on the other side of the next stitch to the left.

6 Go back to the bottom piece of fabric, insert the needle down *into the same place it emerged before*, and bring it up through the middle of the next stitch to the left, connecting the "V" on the piece of fabric at the top to the upside-down "V" on the bottom piece.

7 Repeat these steps until the seam is completed (see illustration below). Cut the yarn, leaving a 6″ tail to be sewn in later.

VERTICAL-TO-HORIZONTAL MATTRESS STITCH SEAMS

This type of seam is useful for setting in the sleeves of garments knitted in stockinette stitch.

1 To make this type of seam, lay the two pieces of fabric flat, with the right sides facing you. Place one piece above the other, orienting the piece at the bottom with the cast-on row at the bottom and the bind-off edge at the top. The piece at the top should be oriented with the cast-on and bind-off edges on either side, perpendicular to the bottom piece.

2 Thread a blunt-end yarn needle with the seaming yarn, leave a 6" tail, and bring the needle up *from back to front* through the center of the first stitch on the right-hand edge of the bottom piece of fabric.

3 On the piece of fabric at the top, insert the needle *from right to left,* catching the running thread (or bar) between the first and second stitches at the right-hand edge of the fabric.

4 Go back to the bottom piece of fabric and insert the needle down *into the same place it emerged before,* then up through the center of the next stitch to the left.

5 Go back to the piece of fabric at the top, insert the needle down *into the same place it emerged before,* and bring it up *from right to left* to catch the next running thread (or bar) between the first and second stitches.

6 Repeat these steps until the seam is completed (see illustration below). Cut the yarn, leaving a 6" tail to be woven in later.

Knit Notes

Because of the difference in dimensions between the stitch gauge and the row gauge in stockinette stitch fabric, you'll occasionally need to go under two bars on the top piece of fabric instead of one. The usual ratio for stockinette stitch is three stitches (on the bottom piece of fabric) for every four rows (on the upper piece).

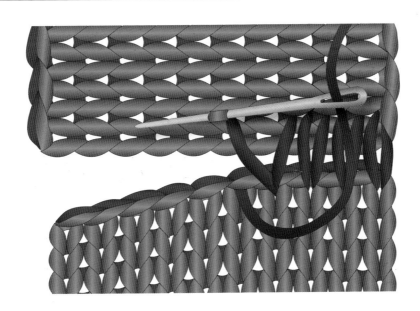

Zippered Jacket

Here's one of those wardrobe basics you'll turn to again and again. The deep ribbing gives it a body-conscious yet extra-comfortable fit. And the textured yarn will hide any sewing imperfections as you practice mattress stitch seams!

SKILL LEVEL
2

BASIC STITCHES AND TECHNIQUES
Gauge
Cable Cast On
Knit Stitch
Purl Stitch
Joining a New Yarn
Knit Two Together Decrease
Slip, Slip, Knit Decrease
Purl Two Together Decrease
Purl Two Together through the Back
    Loops Decrease
Yarn Over Increase
Knitting through the Back Loop
Binding Off
Hiding Yarn Tails
Blocking
Horizontal-to-Horizontal Mattress Stitch
    Seam
Vertical-to-Horizontal Mattress Stitch
    Seam
Vertical-to-Vertical Mattress Stitch Seam

SIZES
Small (Medium, Large, 1X, 2X).
Instructions are for smaller size, with changes for other sizes noted in parentheses as necessary.

FINISHED MEASUREMENTS
Bust (zipped): 34 1/2 (39 1/2, 44, 49 1/2, 54)"
Total length: 20 1/2 (20 1/2, 20 1/2, 22 1/2, 22 1/2)"

MATERIALS
Plymouth Yarn Company's *Alpaca Bouclé* (6-super bulky weight; 90% alpaca/ 10% nylon; each approx 1 3/4 oz/ 60 g and 70 yd/64 m), 15 (17, 18, 19, 20) balls of Autumn Glow #17
One pair *each* of sizes 10, 11, and 13 (6.00, 8.00, and 9.00 mm) knitting needles or size needed to obtain gauge
One size 10 (6.00 mm) circular knitting needle (24" long)
One blunt-end yarn needle
One separating zipper, 18 (18, 18, 20, 20)" long
Sewing thread to match zipper
One pointed-end sewing needle

GAUGE
With smallest needles in Stockinette St Patt, 13 sts and 22 rows = 4". *To save time, take time to check gauge.*

STITCH PATTERNS
K2 P2 Rib Patt
(over mult 4 + 2 sts)
Row 1 (RS): *K2, P2. Repeat from * across, ending row with K2.

Row 2: *P2, K2. Repeat from * across, ending row with P2.

Repeat Rows 1 and 2 for patt.

Stockinette Stitch Pattern
(over any number of sts)
Row 1 (RS): Knit across.

Row 2: Purl across.

Repeat Rows 1 and 2 for patt.

NOTES
For ease in finishing, instructions include one selvage stitch each side; these stitches are not reflected in final measurements.

For fully-fashioned neckline decreases on left side of neck: *on RS rows,* work across until 3 sts rem in row, ending row with K2tog, K1; *on WS rows,* P1, P2tog, then purl across to end row.

For fully-fashioned neckline decreases on right side of neck: *on RS rows,* K1, SSK, then knit across to end row; *on WS rows,* purl across until 3 sts rem in row, ending row with P2tog through back loops, P1.

To prevent holes when increasing for the sleeves, be sure to close up each yarn over increase by knitting it *through its back loop* on the following row.

For sweater assembly, refer to the illustration for square-indented construction on page 126.

BACK

With smallest needles, use cable cast on to CO 58 (66, 74, 82, 90) sts.

Beg K2 P2 Rib Patt, and work even until piece measures approx 7½ (7½, 8, 8, 8)" from beg, ending after WS row.

Beg Stockinette St Patt, and work even until piece measures approx 11½ (11, 10½, 12½, 12)" from beg, ending after WS row.

Shape Armholes

Cont patt as established, and BO 6 (8, 10, 12, 14) sts at beg of next two rows—46 (50, 54, 58, 62) sts rem.

Cont even in patt as established until piece measures approx 19½ (19½, 19½, 21½, 21½)" from beg, ending after WS row.

Shape Shoulders

BO 4 (5, 5, 6, 7) sts at beg of next four rows, then BO 4 (4, 6, 6, 6) sts at beg of next two rows—22 sts rem.

LEFT FRONT

With smallest-sized needles, use cable cast on to CO 30 (34, 38, 42, 46) sts.

Beg K2 P2 Rib Patt, and work even until piece measures approx 7½ (7½, 8, 8, 8)" from beg, ending after WS row.

Beg Stockinette St Patt, and work even until piece measures approx 11½ (11, 10½, 12½, 12)" from beg, ending after WS row.

Shape Armhole

Cont patt as established, and BO 6 (8, 10, 12, 14) sts at beg of next row—24 (26, 28, 30, 32) sts rem.

Cont even in patt as established until piece measures approx 18 (18, 18, 20, 20)" from beg, ending after RS row.

Shape Neck

BO 6 sts at beg of next row—18 (20, 22, 24, 26) sts rem.

Work one row even.

BO 3 sts at beg of next row—15 (17, 19, 21, 23) sts rem.

Dec 1 st at neck edge every row three times, working fully-fashioned decreases for the left side of the neck (see Notes)—12 (14, 16, 18, 20) sts rem.

Cont even in patt as established until piece measures same as back to shoulder, ending after WS row.

Shape Shoulders

BO 4 (5, 5, 6, 7) sts at beg of next row—8 (9, 11, 12, 13) sts rem.

Work one row even.

BO 4 (5, 5, 6, 7) sts at beg of next row—4 (4, 6, 6, 6) sts rem.

Work one row even.

BO.

RIGHT FRONT

Same as left front until piece measures approx 11½ (11, 10½, 12½, 12)" from beg, ending after RS row.

Shape Armhole

Cont patt as established, and BO 6 (8, 10, 12, 14) sts at beg of next row—24 (26, 28, 30, 32) sts rem.

Cont even in patt as established until piece measures approx 18 (18, 18, 20, 20)" from beg, ending after WS row.

Shape Neck

BO 6 sts at beg of next row—18 (20, 22, 24, 26) sts rem.

Work one row even.

BO 3 sts at beg of next row—15 (17, 19, 21, 23) sts rem.

Dec 1 st at neck edge every row three times, working fully-fashioned decreases for the right side of the neck (see Notes)—12 (14, 16, 18, 20) sts rem.

Cont even in patt as established until piece measures same as back to shoulder shaping, ending after RS row.

Shape Shoulders

BO 4 (5, 5, 6, 7) sts at beg of next row—8 (9, 11, 12, 13) sts rem.

Work one row even.

BO 4 (5, 5, 6, 7) sts at beg of next row—4 (4, 6, 6, 6) sts rem.

Work one row even.

BO.

SLEEVE

With smallest needles, use cable cast on to CO 34 sts.

Beg K2 P2 Rib Patt, and work even until piece measures approx 3" from beg, ending after WS row.

Next Row (Inc Row): K2, yarn over, K across until 2 sts rem in row, ending row with yarn over, K2.

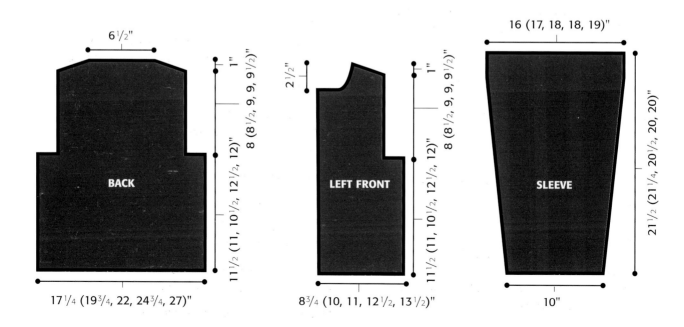

Knit Notes

To sew in a zipper:

1 With the right side of the fabric facing you and the zipper closed, pin the zipper into position. Use contrasting sewing thread to baste the zipper into place and then remove the pins. With matching sewing thread, sew the zipper into place (see illustration 1).

2 Use whipstitch (see page 19) to sew the zipper tape into place (see illustration 2).

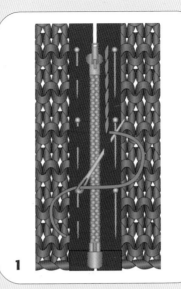

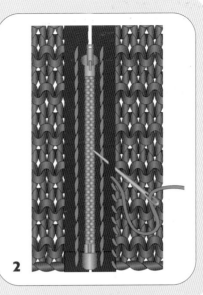

Beg with purl (WS) row, cont Stockinette St Patt as established, and repeat Inc Row every fourth row 0 (0, 0, 2, 7) times, every sixth row 0 (0, 11, 10, 6) times, every eighth row 4 (10, 1, 0, 0) times, then every tenth row 5 (0, 0, 0, 0) times, working into back loop of yarn overs on subsequent rows to prevent holes (see Notes)—54 (56, 60, 60, 52) sts.

Cont even in patt as established until piece measures approx 21½ (21¼, 20½, 20, 20)" from beg.

BO.

FINISHING

Weave in any tails on WS, *except those to be used later in seaming*.

Block pieces to measurements.

Use horizontal-to-horizontal mattress stitch seams to sew shoulder seams.

Collar

With WS facing and smallest needles, beg and end at front edges and pick up and knit 24 sts evenly along right front edge, 22 sts along back of neck, and 24 sts along left front edge—70 sts total.

Beg K2 P2 Rib Patt, and work even until collar measures approx 2½" from beg.

Change to middle-sized needles and cont even in patt as established until collar measures approx 5" from beg.

Change to largest-sized needles and cont even in patt as established until collar measures approx 6½" from beg.

BO *loosely*.

Left Front Edging

With RS facing and circular needle, pick up and knit 52 (52, 52, 56, 56) sts along left side of front opening.

Next Row: Knit and BO.

Right Front Edging

With RS facing and circular needle, pick up and knit 52 (52, 52, 56, 56) sts along left side of front opening.

Next Row: Knit and BO.

Sew in zipper (see "Knit Notes" for instructions).

With RS facing, use vertical-to-horizontal mattress stitch seams to set in sleeves.

With RS facing, use vertical-to-vertical mattress stitch seams to sew sleeve and side seams.

Weave in any remaining yarn tails to WS.

purl stitch decreases, part two

If you think only the knit stitch has a variety of decrease stitches, you're wrong. The purl stitch demands equal attention—and gets it in this lesson!

More Purl Stitch Decreases

Thought there were only a few types of purl decreases? Nope. Here are more, and they'll do the job when you need them.

LEFT-SLANTING PURL STITCH DECREASES

In these decreases, stitches are slipped from the left-hand knitting needle onto the right-hand needle and then back again (in order to set them up with a particular twist) prior to purling them together through their back loops. The maneuver will feel similar—but not quite identical—to the Slip, Slip, Knit and Slip, Slip, Slip Knit Decreases you learned in Lesson 10 on page 72.

Slip, Slip, Purl Decrease

To decrease one stitch while purling and have the resulting stitch slant toward the left on the right side of the fabric, most knitters use the Slip, Slip, Purl Decrease. It's the mirror image of the Purl-Two-Together Decrease.

1 To make this type of decrease, insert the tip of the right-hand needle into the first stitch on the left-hand needle and slip the stitch *knitwise from left to right* onto the right-hand needle (see illustration 1).

2 Likewise, slip the next stitch *knitwise* from the left-hand needle onto the right-hand needle (see illustration 2). It's important that these stitches be slipped *one at a time*.

3 Now slip the two stitches back onto the left-hand needle, *keeping them in the twisted position* (see illustration 3).

4 Finally, position the right-hand needle behind these two slipped stitches. Insert the needle *into the back of the second stitch first and then into the back of the first stitch*. Wrap the yarn around the right-hand needle and purl the two stitches together from this position (see illustration 4).

There, one stitch has been decreased, and on the knit side of the fabric, *the resulting stitch slants to the left*.

Knit Notes

Have you noticed that the Slip, Slip, Purl Decrease is a mirror image of the Purl-Two-Together Decrease? You'll team up these two techniques while knitting the "Tie-Front Cardigan" on page 123 and the "Shaped Pullover" on page 120. It'll make the shaping of these garments look quite beautiful—and make you look like a pro!

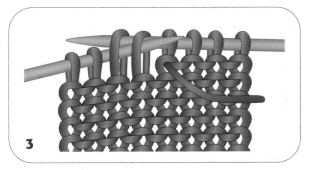

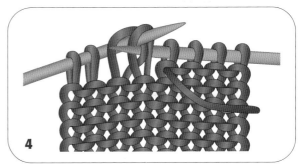

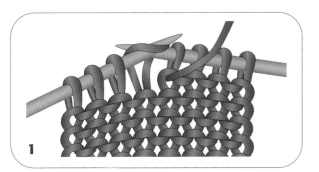

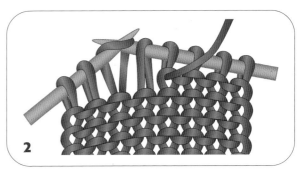

Slip, Slip, Slip, Purl Decrease

This technique is performed on the purl side of the fabric to create a double-decrease (three stitches that become one stitch) and that slants toward the left. The Slip, Slip, Slip, Purl Decrease is made the same way as an Slip, Slip, Purl Decrease, except *three* stitches are slipped onto the right-hand needle instead of two.

1 To begin, insert the tip of the right-hand needle into the first stitch on the left-hand needle *knitwise* and then slip it off onto the right-hand needle (see illustration 1).

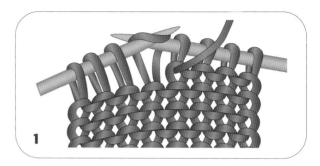

2 Slip the next stitch from the left-hand needle onto the right-hand needle *knitwise* (see illustration 2).

3 Repeat these steps for the next stitch on the left-hand needle—three stitches have been slipped knitwise from the left- to the right-hand needle (see illustration 3). As with the Slip, Slip, Purl Decrease, it's important that these stitches each be slipped knitwise one at a time.

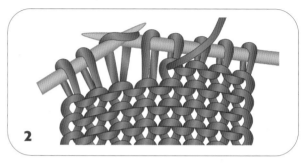

4 Insert the tip of the left-hand needle into the front of all three stitches at once and slip the three stitches back onto the left-hand needle, *keeping them in the twisted position* (see illustration 4).

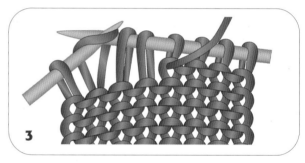

5 Finally, position the right-hand needle behind these three slipped stitches. Insert the needle first into the back of the third stitch, then into the back of the second stitch, and lastly into the back of the first stitch. Wrap the yarn around the right-hand needle and purl the three stitches together from this position (see illustration 5).

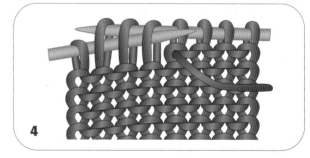

Bravo! Two stitches have been decreased, and on the knit side of the fabric, *the resulting stitch slants toward the left*. The Slip, Slip, Slip Purl Decrease is the perfect mirror image of a Purl Three Together Decrease and is often used opposite it for conspicuous shapings, such as armholes and sleeve caps.

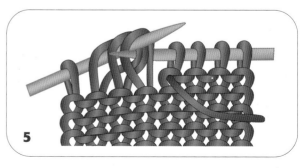

Ribbed Cami

A soft, hand-painted yarn makes this little top extra-special. Thanks to the mirrored decreases, it has beautiful, fully-fashioned shaping details. Plus, for quick and simple finishing, its shoulder straps are incorporated into the knitting of the garment!

SKILL LEVEL
3

BASIC STITCHES AND TECHNIQUES
Gauge
Cable Cast On
Knit Stitch
Purl Stitch
Joining a New Yarn
Alternating between Two Balls of Yarn
Knit Two Together Decrease
Knit Three Together Decrease
Slip, Slip, Knit Decrease
Slip, Slip, Slip, Knit Decrease
Slip, Slip, Purl Decrease
Slip, Slip, Slip, Purl Decrease
Purl Two Together Decrease
Purl Three Together Decrease
Binding Off
Hiding Yarn Tails
Blocking
Vertical-to-Vertical Mattress Stitch Seam

SIZES
Small (Medium, Large, 1X, 2X, 3X).
Instructions are for smallest size, with changes for other sizes noted in parentheses as necessary.

FINISHED MEASUREMENTS
Bust: 30$\frac{1}{2}$ (33$\frac{1}{2}$, 36$\frac{1}{2}$, 39$\frac{1}{2}$, 42, 45$\frac{1}{2}$)"
Length: 20$\frac{1}{2}$ (21, 21$\frac{1}{4}$, 21$\frac{3}{4}$, 22$\frac{1}{4}$, 22$\frac{3}{4}$)"

MATERIALS
Woven Art's *Kona Superwash* (3-DK weight; 100% hand-painted merino wool; each approx 4 oz/110 g and 275 yd/251 m), 2 (3, 3, 3, 4, 4) balls of Larimar

One pair of size 6 (4.00 mm) knitting needles or size needed to obtain gauge
One pair of size 6 (4.00 mm) double-pointed knitting needles or size needed to obtain gauge
One blunt-end yarn needle

GAUGE
In Ribbed Patt, 27 sts and 28 rows = 4".
To save time, take time to check gauge.

STITCH PATTERNS
Ribbed Pattern
(over mult 10 + 3 sts)
Row 1 (RS): *K3, P3, K1, P3. Repeat from * across, ending row with K3.

Row 2: *P3, K3, P1, K3. Repeat from * across, ending row with P3.

Repeat Rows 1 and 2 for patt.

I-cord Pattern *(a knitted tube)*
(over 3 sts)
Row 1 (RS): K3. *Do not turn.*

Row 2 (RS): Slide sts to right-hand end of needle and K3.

Repeat Row 2 for patt.

NOTES
To decrease one stitch each side: *on RS rows,* K3, P3, SSK, work across in patt as established until 8 sts rem in row, ending row with K2tog, P3, K3; *on WS rows,* P3, K3, P2tog, work across in patt as established until 8 sts rem in row, ending row with SSP, K3, P3.

To decrease two stitches each side: *on RS rows,* K3, P3, SSSK, work across in patt as established until 9 sts rem, ending row with K3tog, P3, K3; *on WS rows,* P3, K3, P3tog, work across in patt as established until 9 sts rem in row, ending row with SSSP, K3, P3.

For even color distribution in this hand-dyed yarn, alternate between two balls of yarn, working two rows from one ball, then two rows from the second ball, carrying the unused yarn *loosely* along side of work on WS; when knitting the shoulder straps, do not alternate between two balls of yarn.

BACK

Use cable cast on to CO 103 (113, 123, 133, 143, 153) sts.

Beg Ribbed Patt, and work even until piece measures approx 12 (12$\frac{1}{4}$, 12$\frac{1}{4}$, 12$\frac{1}{4}$, 12$\frac{1}{4}$, 12$\frac{1}{4}$)" from beg, or until desired length, ending after WS row.

Shape Armholes

Dec 1 st each side (see Notes) every other row 1 (0, 0, 0, 0, 0) times, dec 1 st each side every row 19 (21, 20, 21, 24, 25) times, then dec 2 sts each side (see Notes) every row 0 (2, 5, 7, 8, 10) times, ending after WS row—63 sts rem.

BO, knitting the knit sts and purling the purl sts as you go.

FRONT

Same as back. *Do not BO.*

Shoulder Straps

Next Row (RS): K3, BO middle 57 sts in patt, K2—3 sts rem each side.

Change to dpns and work I-cord Patt on each group of 3 sts until straps measure approx 10$\frac{3}{4}$" from beg, or until desired length.

BO.

FINISHING

Weave in any tails on WS, *except those to be used later in seaming*.

Block pieces to measurements.

Knit Notes

This ribbed garment is designed with "negative ease." This means that the finished knitted measurements for each size are smaller than the actual body measurements to create a body-conscious fit. But don't worry—the ribbed fabric has plenty of give for comfort. When choosing which size to knit, select the same one you would normally choose for other garments.

With RS facing, use vertical-to-vertical mattress stitch seams to sew side seams.

With RS facing, use vertical-to-vertical mattress stitch seams to sew shoulder straps to back.

Weave in any remaining yarn tails to WS.

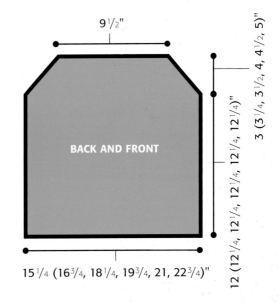

9$\frac{1}{2}$"

BACK AND FRONT

3 (3$\frac{1}{4}$, 3$\frac{1}{2}$, 4, 4$\frac{1}{2}$, 5)"

12 (12$\frac{1}{4}$, 12$\frac{1}{4}$, 12$\frac{1}{4}$, 12$\frac{1}{4}$, 12$\frac{1}{4}$)"

15$\frac{1}{4}$ (16$\frac{3}{4}$, 18$\frac{1}{4}$, 19$\frac{3}{4}$, 21, 22$\frac{3}{4}$)"

another type of increase

In Lesson 9 on page 66, you learned the Yarn Over Increase, which creates a hole in the fabric unless you twist the yarn over the stitch on the subsequent row. Here you'll make an invisible increase that can be completed in a single row.

Make One Increase

To make an invisible increase that can be completed in a single row, use the Make One Increase. With this type of increase, a stitch is worked *between* stitches rather than into them. It's easy once you learn how!

1 To do this kind of increase, use the left-hand needle to scoop up the horizontal strand of yarn that's lying between the left- and right-hand knitting needles *from front to back* (see illustration 1).

2 Then knit the strand *through the back loop* (see illustration 2).

Knitting it through the back loop twists the stitch and prevents a hole from forming in the fabric.

Knit Notes

The Make One Increase I've described here slants toward the left on the right side of the fabric. If you'd like to do the mirror image and have your Make One Increase slant toward the right, then scoop up that same horizontal strand that's lying between the two knitting needles *from back to front* and then knit it *through the front loop*. The combination of these two techniques will make your sleeve increases beautiful (even if you're the only one who will ever see them)!

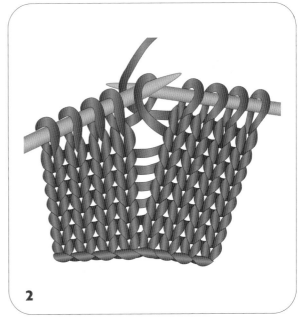

1

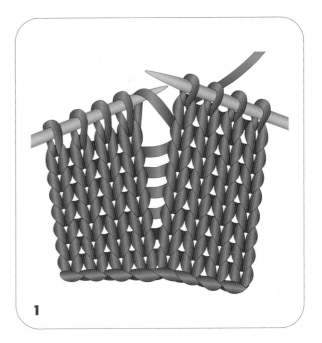

2

Shaped Pullover

Fine couture details such as interior waist shaping, neatly set-in sleeves, and an integrated V-neckline make this sweater particularly flattering. You'll use the Make One Increase for invisible one-step increases as you knit the sleeves.

SKILL LEVEL
3

BASIC STITCHES AND TECHNIQUES
Gauge
Cable Cast On
Knit Stitch
Purl Stitch
Joining a New Yarn
Knit Two Together Decrease
Slip, Slip, Knit Decrease
Slip, Slip, Purl Decrease
Purl Two Together Decrease
Make One Increase
Binding Off
Hiding Yarn Tails
Blocking
Horizontal-to-Horizontal Mattress Stitch
  Seam
Vertical-to-Horizontal Mattress Stitch
  Seam
Vertical-to-Vertical Mattress Stitch Seam

SIZES
Small (Medium, Large, 1X, 2X).
Instructions are for smallest size, with changes for other sizes noted in parentheses as necessary.

FINISHED MEASUREMENTS
Bust: 34 (38, 42, 46, 50)"
Length: $22^{1}/_{2}$ (23, 23, $23^{1}/_{2}$, $23^{1}/_{2}$)"

MATERIALS
Aurora Yarns/Ornaghi Filati's *Super Merino* (4-worsted weight; 65% superwash merino wool/35% acrylic; each approx $1^{3}/_{4}$ oz/50 g and 83 yd/75 m), 11 (12, 13, 13, 14) balls of Sweet Plum #742
One pair of size 10 (6.00 mm) knitting needles or size needed to obtain gauge
Two stitch markers
One blunt-end yarn needle

GAUGE
In Stockinette St Patt, 16 sts and 20 rows = 4". *To save time, take time to check gauge.*

STITCH PATTERNS
K2 P2 Rib Pattern
(over mult 4 + 2 sts)
Row 1 (RS): *K2, P2. Repeat from * across, ending row with K2.

Row 2: *P2, K2. Repeat from * across, ending row with P2.

Repeat Rows 1 and 2 for patt.

Stockinette Stitch Pattern
(over any number of sts)
Row 1 (RS): Knit across.

Row 2: Purl across.

Repeat Rows 1 and 2 for patt.

NOTES
For ease in finishing, instructions include one selvage st each side; these sts are not reflected in final measurements.

For fully-fashioned decreases: *on RS rows,* K2, SSK, work across in patt as established until 4 sts rem in row, ending row with K2tog, K2; *on WS rows,* P2, P2tog, work across in patt as established until 4 sts rem in row, ending row with SSP, P2.

For fully-fashioned increases on sleeves: K2, M1, work across in patt as established until 2 sts rem, ending row with M1, K2.

For sweater assembly, refer to the illustration for set-in construction on page 126.

Knit Notes
For a longer version of this (or any) sweater, simply knit additional rows *before beginning the armhole shaping.* If you mistakenly add them higher up in the garment, the sleeve caps won't fit into the armholes!

BACK

Use cable cast on to CO 70 (78, 86, 94, 102) sts.

Beg K2 P2 Rib Patt, and work even until piece measures approx 2" from beg, ending after WS row.

Beg Stockinette St Patt, and work even for six rows.

Decrease for Waist

Next Row (RS): K13 (17, 21, 25, 29) sts, SSK, place stitch marker, K40, place marker, K2tog, K13 (17, 21, 25, 29) sts to end row—68 (76, 84, 92, 100) sts rem.

Work five rows even.

Next Row (Dec Row): Knit across until 2 sts rem before first marker, SSK, slip marker, knit across until next marker, slip marker, K2tog, knit across to end row—66 (74, 82, 90, 98) sts rem.

Repeat Dec Row every sixth row two more times—62 (70, 78, 86, 94) sts rem.

Cont even until piece measures approx 9" from beg, ending after WS row.

Increase for Bust

Next Row (RS) (Inc Row): Knit across to first marker, slip marker, M1, knit across to next marker, M1, slip marker, knit across to end row—64 (72, 80, 88, 96) sts.

Repeat Inc Row every sixth row three more times—70 (78, 86, 94, 102) sts.

Remove markers, and cont even until piece measures approx 13" from beg, ending after WS row.

Shape Armholes

BO 3 (4, 5, 6, 7) at beg of next 2 rows, then BO 2 (2, 3, 4, 4) sts at beg of next two rows—60 (66, 70, 74, 80) sts rem.

Work fully-fashioned decrease (see Notes) each side on next row, then every row 1 (1, 3, 3, 7) times, then every other row 4 (6, 5, 6, 4) times—48 (50, 52, 54, 56) sts rem.

Cont even until piece measures approx 21 (21½, 21½, 22, 22)" from beg, ending after WS row.

Next Row (RS): K5 (6, 7, 8, 9) sts, [P2, K2] nine times, P2, K5 (6, 7, 8, 9) sts to end row.

Next Row (WS): P5 (6, 7, 8, 9) sts, [K2, P2] nine times, K2, P5 (6, 7, 8, 9) sts to end row.

Shape Shoulders

Cont even in patts as established, BO 4 (4, 5, 5, 5) sts at beg of next four rows, then BO 4 (5, 4, 5, 6) sts at beg of next two rows.

BO rem 24 sts in patt.

FRONT

Same as back until piece measures approx 16¼ (16¾, 16¾, 17¼, 17¼)" from beg, ending after RS row.

Next Row (WS): P16 (17, 18, 19, 20) sts, place marker, P16, place marker, P16 (17, 18, 19, 20) sts to end row.

Shape Neck

Next Row (RS) (Dec Row): Knit across until 2 sts rem before first marker, K2tog, slip marker, K1, P2, K2, P2, K1; join second ball of yarn and K1, P2, K2, P2, K1, slip marker, SSK, knit across to end row.

Work both sides at once with separate balls of yarn, and repeat Dec Row every other row nine more times, then every fourth row two times—12 (13, 14, 15, 16) sts rem each side.

Cont even until piece measures same as back to shoulders.

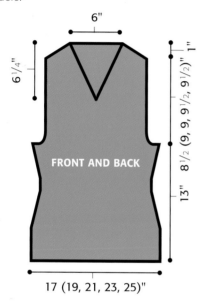

Shape Shoulders

Work both sides at once with separate balls of yarn, and BO 4 (4, 5, 5, 5) sts at beg of next two rows, then BO 4 (5, 4, 5, 6) sts at beg of next two rows.

SLEEVES

Use cable cast on to CO 38 sts.

Beg K2 P2 Rib Patt, and work even in patts as established until piece measures approx 2" from beg, ending after WS row.

Beg Stockinette St Patt, and work fully-fashioned increases (see Notes) each side on next row, then every fourth row 0 (0, 0, 3, 3) times, every sixth row 7 (10, 10, 10, 10) times, then every eighth row 3 (1, 1, 0, 0) times—60 (62, 62, 66, 66) sts.

Cont even until piece measures approx 17½ (18, 18, 18½, 18½)" from beg, ending after WS row.

Shape Cap

BO 3 (4, 5, 6, 7) sts at beg of next two rows—54 (54, 52, 54, 52) sts rem.

Work fully-fashioned decreases (see Notes) each side every other row 6 (9, 10, 11, 12) times, then every row 11 (8, 6, 6, 4) times—20 sts rem.

BO 2 sts at beg of next four rows—12 sts rem.

BO.

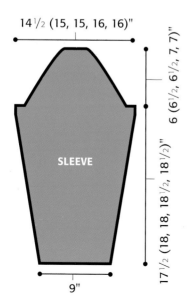

FINISHING

Weave in any tails on WS, *except those to be used later in seaming.*

Block pieces to measurements.

With RS facing, use horizontal-to-horizontal mattress stitch seams to sew shoulder seams.

With RS facing, use a combination of vertical-to-horizontal and vertical-to-vertical mattress stitch seams to set in sleeves.

With RS facing, use vertical-to-vertical mattress stitch seams to sew sleeve and side seams.

Weave in any remaining yarn tails to WS.

Tie-Front Cardigan

You'll love knitting—and wearing!—this sweater, which is made with one of the softest yarns imaginable. While knitting it, you'll use most of the techniques presented in the lessons of this book.

SKILL LEVEL
3

BASIC STITCHES AND TECHNIQUES
Gauge
Cable Cast On
Knit Stitch
Purl Stitch
Joining a New Yarn
Knit Two Together Decrease
Knit Three Together Decrease
Slip, Slip, Knit Decrease
Slip, Slip, Purl Decrease
Purl Two Together Decrease
Make One Increase
Binding Off
Hiding Yarn Tails
Blocking
Horizontal-to-Horizontal Mattress Stitch Seam
Vertical-to-Horizontal Mattress Stitch Seam
Vertical-to-Vertical Mattress Stitch Seam

SIZES
Extra-Small (Small, Medium, Large, 1X, 2X, 3X). *Instructions are for smallest size, with changes for other sizes noted in parentheses as necessary.*

FINISHED MEASUREMENTS
Bust: 32 (35, 37½, 40, 43, 46, 50)"
Length: 15 (15½, 16, 16½, 16½, 16¾, 16¾)"

MATERIALS
Plymouth Yarn Company's *Baby Alpaca Brush* (5-bulky weight; 80% baby alpaca/20% acrylic; each approx 1¾ oz/50 g and 110 yd/101 m), 5 (6, 6, 7, 7, 8, 8) balls of Spring Green #1477

One pair of size 9 (5.50 mm) knitting needles or size needed to obtain gauge
One blunt-end yarn needle

GAUGE
In Stockinette St Patt, 18 sts and 24 rows = 4". *To save time, take time to check gauge.*

STITCH PATTERNS
Stockinette Stitch Pattern
(over any number of sts)
Row 1 (RS): Knit across.

Row 2: Purl across.

Repeat Rows 1 and 2 for patt.

K1 P1 Rib Stitch Pattern
(over mult of 2 sts)
Row 1 (RS): *K1, P1. Repeat from * across.

Row 2: *P1, K1. Repeat from * across.

Repeat Rows 1 and 2 for patt.

NOTES
For ease in finishing, instructions include one selvage stitch each side; these stitches are not reflected in final measurements.

For fully-fashioned decreases: *on RS rows,* K2, SSK, work across in patt as established until 4 sts rem in row, ending row with K2tog, K2; *on WS rows,* P2, P2tog, work across in patt as established until 4 sts rem in row, ending row with SSP, P2.

For fully-fashioned increases: K2, M1, work across in patt as established until 2 sts rem in row, ending row with M1, K2.

For sweater assembly, refer to the illustration for set-in construction on page 126.

Knit Notes
Make yourself a "cheat sheet" to help keep track of the increases and decreases for this cardigan. Write down every row, indicating any shaping to be done. Then mark off each row with a checkmark once it's knitted.

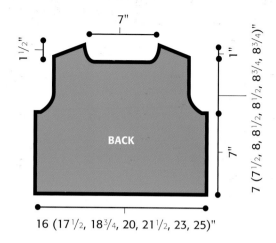

7"

1½"

BACK

1"

7 (7½, 8, 8½, 8½, 8¾, 8¾)"

7"

16 (17½, 18¾, 20, 21½, 23, 25)"

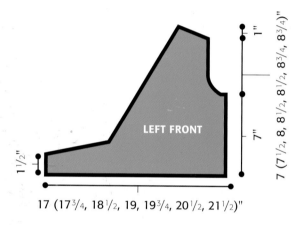

1"

7 (7½, 8, 8½, 8½, 8¾, 8¾)"

7"

LEFT FRONT

1½"

17 (17¾, 18½, 19, 19¾, 20½, 21½)"

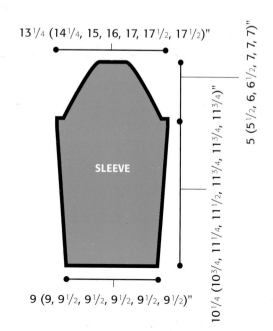

13¼ (14¼, 15, 16, 17, 17½, 17½)"

5 (5½, 6, 6½, 7, 7, 7)"

SLEEVE

10¼ (10¾, 11¼, 11½, 11¾, 11¾, 11¾)"

9 (9, 9½, 9½, 9½, 9½, 9½)"

BACK

Use cable cast on to CO 74 (80, 86, 92, 98, 106, 114) sts.

Beg Stockinette St Patt, and work even until piece measures approx 7" from beg, ending after WS row.

Shape Armholes

BO 2 (2, 3, 4, 4, 5, 6) sts at beg of next two rows—70 (76, 78, 84, 90, 96, 102) sts rem.

Work fully-fashioned decreases (see Notes) each side on next row, then every row 0 (2, 2, 4, 4, 6, 10) times, every other row 1 (3, 4, 4, 7, 9, 8) times, then every fourth row 3 (2, 2, 2, 1, 0, 0) times—60 (60, 62, 62, 64, 64, 64) sts rem.

Cont even until piece measures approx 13½ (14, 14½, 15, 15, 15¼, 15¼)" from beg, ending after WS row.

Shape Neck

Work across first 15 (15, 16, 16, 17, 17, 17) sts; join second ball of yarn and BO middle 30 sts, work across to end row.

Work both sides at once with separate balls of yarn, and dec 1 st each neck edge once.

Cont even until piece measures approx 14 (14½, 15, 15½, 15½, 15¾, 15¾)" from beg, ending after WS row.

Shape Shoulders

BO 5 sts at beg of next four rows, then BO 4 (4, 5, 5, 6, 6, 6) sts at beg of next two rows.

LEFT FRONT

Use cable cast on to CO 78 (82, 86, 88, 90, 94, 98) sts.

Beg Stockinette St Patt, and work even until piece measures approx 1½" from beg, ending after WS row.

Shape Ties

BO 8 sts at neck edge two times, BO 6 sts at neck edge once, BO 4 sts at neck edge once, then BO 2 sts at neck edge once—50 (54, 58, 60, 62, 66, 70) sts rem.

Shape Neck and Armholes

Work fully-fashioned decrease (see Notes) at neck edge on next row, then every other row 26 (26, 27, 23, 21, 20, 20) times, then every fourth row 2 (3, 3, 6, 7, 8, 8) times, **and at the same time,** when piece measures same as back to armholes, BO 2 (2, 3, 4, 4, 5, 6) sts at armhole edge once, then dec 1 st at armhole edge every row 1 (3, 3, 5, 5, 7, 11) times, every other row 1 (3, 4, 4, 7, 9, 8) times, then every fourth row 3 (2, 2, 2, 1, 0, 0) times—14 (14, 15, 15, 16, 16, 16) sts rem.

Cont even until piece measures same as back to shoulder, ending after WS row.

Shape Shoulder

BO 5 sts at beg of next row—9 (9, 10, 10, 11, 11, 11) sts rem.

Work one row even.

BO 5 sts at beg of next row—4 (4, 5, 5, 6, 6, 6) sts rem.

Work one row even.

BO.

RIGHT FRONT

Same as left front *except* reverse all shaping.

SLEEVE

Use cable cast on to CO 42 (42, 44, 44, 44, 44, 44) sts.

Work K1 P1 Rib Patt for four rows.

Beg Stockinette St Patt, and work fully-fashioned increases (see Notes) each side on next row, then every other row 0 (0, 0, 1, 4, 6, 6) times, every fourth row 4 (9, 7, 13, 12, 11, 11) times, then every sixth row 5 (2, 4, 0, 0, 0, 0) times—62 (66, 68, 74, 78, 80, 80) sts.

Cont even until piece measures approx 10$\frac{1}{4}$ (10$\frac{3}{4}$, 11$\frac{1}{4}$, 11$\frac{1}{2}$, 11$\frac{3}{4}$, 11$\frac{3}{4}$, 11$\frac{3}{4}$)" from beg.

Shape Cap

BO 2 (2, 3, 4, 4, 5, 6) sts at beg of next two rows—58 (62, 62, 66, 70, 70, 68) sts rem.

Work fully-fashioned decreases (see Notes) each side on next row, then every other row 2 (3, 6, 7, 8, 8, 9) times, then every row 17 (18, 15, 16, 17, 17, 15) times—18 sts rem.

BO 2 sts at beg of next four rows—10 sts rem.

BO.

FINISHING

Weave in any tails on WS, *except those to be used later in seaming.*

Block pieces to measurements.

With RS facing, use horizontal-to-horizontal mattress stitch seams to sew shoulder seams.

With RS facing, use a combination of vertical-to-horizontal and vertical-to-vertical mattress stitch seams to set in sleeves.

With RS facing, use vertical-to-vertical mattress stitch seams to sew sleeve and side seams.

Weave in any remaining yarn tails to WS.

Congratulations! That's twenty-one wardrobe-ready fashions in just sixteen easy knitting lessons! So what are you going to make next? You've mastered the two basic stitches of this fun, time-loved craft as well as various shaping techniques using them. There's nothing you can't try now! Just go for it!

Sweater Assembly

Pieces for knitted garments fit together like a jigsaw puzzle, with the type of armhole determining how the front, back, and sleeves interlock. Refer to the drawings below when assembling sweaters.

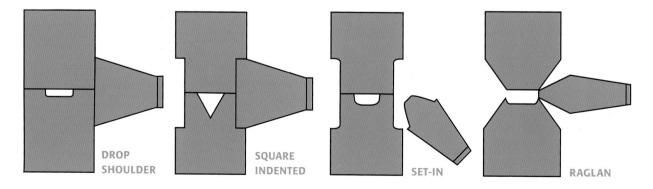

DROP SHOULDER

SQUARE INDENTED

SET-IN

RAGLAN

Material Resources

MANUFACTURERS

These companies sell wholesale only. Contact them to locate retail stores in your area.

Artful Yarns
see JCA, Inc.

Aurora Yarns
P.O. Box 3068
Moss Beach, CA 94038
(650) 728-8554
www.garnstudio.com

Berroco, Inc.
14 Elmdale Road
P.O. Box 367
Uxbridge, MA 01569
(508) 278-2527
www.berroco.com

Classic Elite Yarns
122 Western Avenue
Lowell, MA 01851
(978) 453-2837
www.classiceliteyarns.com

JCA, Inc.
35 Scales Lane
Townsend, MA 01469
(978) 597-8794
www.jcacrafts.com

JHB International, Inc.
1955 South Quince Street
Denver, CO 80231
(303) 751-8100
www.buttons.com

Judi & Co.
18 Gallatin Drive
Dix Hills, NY 11746
(631) 499-8480
www.judiandco.com

Knit One, Crochet Too
91 Tandberg Trail
Unit 6
Windham, ME 04062
(207) 892-9625
www.knitonecrochettoo.com

Kraemer Yarns
P.O. Box 72
Nazareth, PA 18064
(800) 759-5601
www.kraemeryarnshop.com

Lorna's Laces
4229 North Honore Street
Chicago, IL 60613
(773) 935-3803
www.lornaslaces.net

Ornaghi Filati
see Aurora Yarns

Plymouth Yarn Company
500 Lafayette Street
P.O. Box 28
Bristol, PA 19007
(215) 788-0459
www.plymouthyarn.com

Reynolds Yarn
see JCA, Inc.

South West Trading Company
918 South Park Lane
Suite 102
Tempe, AZ 85281
(480) 894-1818
www.soysilk.com

Trendsetter Yarns
16745 Saticoy Street, #101
Van Nuys, CA 91406
(818) 780-5497
www.trendsetteryarns.com

Unique Kolours
28 North Bacton Hill Road
Malvern, PA 19355
(610) 644-4885
www.uniquekolours.com

Woven Art
325-B Grove Street
East Lansing, MI 48823
(517) 203-4467
www.mcrayweaving.com

MAIL ORDER AND INTERNET YARN SOURCES

Patternworks
Route 25
P.O. Box 1618
Center Harbor, NH 03226
(800) 438-5464
www.patternworks.com

Wool Connection
34 East Main Street
Avon, CT 06001
(800) 933-9665
www.woolconnection.com

THE KNITTING GUILD ASSOCIATION

To meet other knitters and to learn more about the craft, contact:

The Knitting Guild Association
1100-H Brandywine Boulevard
Zanesville, OH 43701
(740) 452-4541
E-mail: tkga@tkga.com
Web site: www.tkga.com

Index